DOWN
THE
RUNWAY

The Making of a Pilot

Samuel Hawkins

Cover and illustrations by George Grant

TAB TAB BOOKS Inc.
Blue Ridge Summit, PA

FIRST EDITION
FIRST PRINTING

Copyright © 1989 by TAB BOOKS Inc.
Printed in the United States of America

Library of Congress Cataloging in Publication Data

Hawkins, Samuel.
    Down the runway : the making of a pilot / by Samuel Hawkins.
    p. cm.
    ISBN 0-8306-2425-2 (pbk.)
    1. Hawkins, Samuel.   2. Air pilots—United States—Biography.
I. Title.
TL540.H338H39 1988
629.13'092'4—dc19   88-25036
[B]   CIP

TAB BOOKS Inc. offers software for sale. For information and a catalog, please contact TAB Software Department, Blue Ridge Summit, PA 17294-0850.

Questions regarding the content of this book should be addressed to:

    Reader Inquiry Branch
    TAB BOOKS Inc.
    Blue Ridge Summit, PA 17294-0214

CONTENTS

TO THE NONPILOT   v

ACKNOWLEDGMENTS   vi

1 // BO WAGES   1

2 // WAITING   8

3 // BO'S PLAN   13

4 // SEVEN DAYS WITHOUT BILLY   18

5 // UNEXPECTED HELP   23

6 // FRANKLIN'S BIG EVENT   32

7 // TEXAS WIND   37

8 // UFO IN SOUTH TEXAS   41

9 // MURPHY'S LAW   44

10 // THUNDERSTORM IN THE CACTUS   50

11 // FIRST FLIGHT   57

12 // MY SPECIAL TAILGUNNER   64

13 // THE COST OF FLYING   84

14 // BUSTER'S BIRD DOG   89

15 // FUNDAMENTALS   94

16 // THE LAST MISSION   97

17 // SOBERING UP   122

18 // SOLO   126

19 // AIR, WIND, AND WEATHER   129

20 // A MEDAL FOR OLD SOGGY   134

21 // RAINMAKER   143

TO THE NONPILOT

THIS BOOK IS WRITTEN IN THE LANGUAGE OF AVIation. This language has its own unique set of abbreviations, acronyms, and slang. It is only natural that many of the words and phrases in this book will be foreign to the nonpilot. I encourage those of you who are new to this language to ask a pilot friend to translate for you. Better yet, visit your local airport. Seek out and get to know a good airport operator. He is a man in love with aviation and in the business of aviation. He will welcome you and gladly provide assistance that will extend beyond a few new words.

ACKNOWLEDGMENTS

A LTHOUGH THIS BOOK DRAWS HEAVILY ON PER-
sonal experiences, it was especially difficult for me to write.
The art of assembling experiences into coherent and
meaningful narratives is that of the writer. I am a pilot. There were
times in its development when I put it aside with the promise to
try again—knowing full well that I might never return to the work.
Fortunately, at each of these critical times, a friend would appear
to help and encourage me. This book would not have been
completed without their help.

Originally, my intention was to assemble instructive and
entertaining experiences into a series of magazine articles, but the
results were disappointing. Discouraged, I drifted away from the
work. It might have ended there except for my good friend George
Chatham from the Library of Congress, who is also Aeronautical
Advisor to the U.S. Senate. George reviewed my early work,
encouraged me to continue, and suggested a book, rather than
magazine articles.

Soon after George's suggestion, the conceptual aspects of the book were complete. I began the more difficult task of transforming ideas into written words and soon found myself mired in the structural details. The dilemma was a simple one. I knew what I wanted to relate to the reader, but lacked the skill to put it onto typewritten pages. Laboring at great length with sentence structure, dialogue, paragraphing, and other writer skills foreign to me, I wearied myself arranging, rearranging, writing, and rewriting. Exhausted, I again pushed the work aside and concluded that I lacked the energy to write a book.

At this point, I happened to fly Elder Cyril Miller, my friend and president of The Texas Conference of Seventh Day Adventists, to address a group of elderly persons in another city. As a perchance listener to Cyril's words to those old folks whose health was poor, I found that his message applied equally well to me. He advised us to believe, to pray, and to try. Believe in yourself and what you can do. Pray for help and guidance. Above all, try, try, and try. Do not give in to weakness, difficulty, or discouragement, but continue trying. I returned to the book with renewed confidence and energy.

This book, being mostly about flying and people who fly, could not have been written without my lifelong love affair with aviation. No aviation career proceeds without some involvement with the Federal Aviation Administration (FAA), formerly the Civil Aeronautics Administration (CAA). In numerous places along the way in my career, I was helped by the CAA and later the FAA. But two persons in particular stand out in my memory.

During the difficult times between wars, when aviation was supposed to boom but went broke instead, many people abandoned aviation in favor of jobs that paid a living wage. During the lean years of 1947 and 1948, I was tempted to seek another career. In fact, I had good offers for nonaviation employment that I would have accepted had it not been for "Pop" Schneider, a CAA pilot examiner. Pop was a kind old gentleman ready to retire from government service when I met him in 1947. He had flown in World War I and barnstormed after. Later, he flew as part of an aerial circus. He served his country again during World War II as a flight instructor. He had a pilot's certificate signed by Orville Wright—not rubber-stamped, but actually signed. He kept me in aviation by pure magnetism.

As the years passed, the world of flying became more delineated with rules, regulations, policies, procedures, and court cases. My view of aviation became negative. I felt that a pilot needed to be a lawyer before becoming a pilot, and that this oppressive maze of restrictive entanglements was to be avoided or even turned against itself. This view was driving me toward rejection of the system and eventually toward violation of aviation regulations.

At this time, when all the rules seemed aimed directly at me and designed to limit my participation in aviation, at a time when my romance with aviation was being severely tested, came Annabelle Stone, FAA operations inspector and superb pilot. In her quiet and friendly way, Annabelle smoothed a path through several difficult periods and created an environment in which I learned that our operating system today is an outgrowth of experience in aviation safety. She succeeded in reversing my negative view and thus restored my love for aviation.

In beginning this work, I visualized a writer as one who could sit at a typewriter and write a story, at least in good draft form, from scratch. I am not capable of such a feat. This fact did not, and does not now, bother me because I see myself as a pilot, not as a writer. Accordingly, this book was written in brief fits of rabid activity at the time and place when a fresh idea struck. It was scribbled on the backs of maps in cockpits thousands of feet in the air. It was scratched on paper napkins while waiting in airport coffee shops. It was penciled and inked on the backs of envelopes while waiting for the important people who make my job possible.

As the collection of assorted bits of paper and ideas massed, I blended, shuffled, altered, rearranged, and finally gave them to the only person who could produce an orderly manuscript from such chaos: Sharon Lunsford. Sharon is a professional, who craftily transformed my difficult draft, with its many scribbled notes, into a secretarial work of art.

Although there have been important characters who have walked on and off the stage at critical times during the running of my play called "writing a book," there was one player who had a paramount role from beginning to end: my dear wife Betty Ann. Quietly enduring my indifference to her needs, she continually supported and encouraged me.

In view of the help and encouragement without which this book would not have been completed, it is dedicated to George, Cyril, "Pop," Annabelle, Sharon and, with love, to my beautiful wife, Betty Ann.

BO WAGES

IN THE SUMMER OF 1933, BO WAGES RAN OUT OF GAS in his homemade airplane. It was probably not the first time that had happened. Bo had a little bit of the gambler in him and would take a chance now and then. It certainly wasn't the last time he went down with dry tanks, but this particular time was important to me because the events that followed led me into flying and shaped the rest of my life.

Bo was working his way across Texas that year by giving airplane rides and teaching a little flying. Somehow, he never stayed in one place long enough for any of his students to solo his biplane—and that was probably a good thing since it was a difficult airplane to fly. With power on, it had to be forced into every turn and then held there. It had to be pounded, shoved, and kicked into every maneuver attempted. The control forces were exhausting. On the other hand, with power off, it was totally unstable and nearly impossible to control. Just maintaining a straight descent without power required the pilot to madly manipulate the stick to

1

all four corners of the cockpit while thrashing wildly on the rudders. The cockpit of that airplane was no place for a timid student on his first solo flight.

A year earlier, Bo had built that odd-looking machine out of bits and pieces from a dozen different airplanes. It just grew bit by bit as pieces became available and were adapted to fit. No one could say what size engine the airplane would require because its building followed no particular plan. However, the general size and shape of the machine seemed to call for 90 horsepower or more.

Being without means, Bo had no prospects of buying a suitable engine. According to Bo, the good Lord himself solved the puzzle when one of our fierce Texas thunderstorms dumped about a ton of baseball-sized hail on his employer's new Ford Coupe. A local farmer bought the chassis, axles, and wheels, from which he built a fine trailer. Bo got the engine in exchange for some overtime work. So the boxy biplane got a tiny 60-horsepower Ford V8 engine, for which Bo promptly whittled a six-foot propeller.

This odd-looking, underpowered, difficult-to-fly machine, with Bo in the rear cockpit and all of his belongings in the front, came clattering into my boyhood skies on a cloudless, late-August afternoon. The day was dry and hot. There was no motion in the air. The stillness was absolute. Each step across the dry dirt floor of our dairy barn stirred a small cloud of dust. It was so still that I imagined I could hear the aroused dust particles falling back to the floor. Each stream of milk that I squeezed from the cow ripped the silence and roared into the bucket I held between my knees.

Although airplanes were far from my thoughts, I had been in love with them since my father had taken two of his hard-earned Depression dollars to buy tickets to the air show at Galveston a year earlier. It had been a spectacular air show. I had been mesmerized by parachute jumps, all manner of aerobatics, and a passenger's daring plane-to-plane transfer.

Those were the only airplanes I had actually seen in flight, but I could detect and identify airplane sounds from miles away. On this still afternoon, that unmistakable sound that says "airplane" drifted lightly through the dairy barn. The sound grew stronger.

Deserting the cow that I was milking, I ran out of the barn and searched the skies, fearing that I might miss this important event. I did a quick turn searching for the source of that wonderful noise. There it was! At no more than 500 or 600 feet in altitude, the airplane was flying directly toward me. It looked odd with its large radiator standing erect between the fuselage and the upper wing, directly in front of the open front cockpit. Little did I realize then how that enormous restriction to forward visibility would confound my early attempts at airmanship.

Now that it was directly overhead, I could see the airplane's underside and the shape of the wings. Then suddenly, the engine gave two strong bursts and fell silent. It surged to life again, only to sputter into silence once more. "His engine's quit," I thought.

"His engine's quit!" I shouted aloud as the importance of what was happening came to me. I could see the pilot struggling at the controls. In fact, I could see the control surfaces themselves flailing up and down, and back and forth, as the biplane turned back toward our pasture. He was going to land in our pasture.

"He's going to land in our pasture!" I excitedly blurted to a nonexistent group of onlookers.

Running toward the pasture, I watched the pilot battling for a few more seconds of control as he neared the ground. The right wheel struck with a loud "Whump," and the biplane rebounded into the air. It rolled to its left, and the left wingtip dug into the pasture soil. As the wing dug deeper, the airplane started to cartwheel. The windmilling propeller thrashed against the earth, and the whole machine rose up on its nose, then skidded for some distance, and crashed down on its back. Resting on its back, with wheels pointed skyward, the biplane looked humorously like a dead chicken, I thought.

When I reached the airplane, the pilot was suspended above the ground still strapped tightly in his seat with his helmet and goggles in place. He was cursing loudly and pounding on the instrument panel.

"You all right, mister?" I asked.

Taking a deep breath and exhaling slowly, he looked me squarely in the eye. A broad grin slowly snuck from behind his large bushy mustache, and he asked, "You wouldn't happen to have a couple of gallons of gas you could lend a fellow, do you?"

"Well, sir, I really don't think you could use it because you broke your wing and bent your tail thing back there."

"Tail thing?" he almost shouted. "Tail thing?" he repeated. Raising his goggles and squinting his eyes to emphasize his seriousness and overcome his upside-downness, he scolded,

"Vertical fin, boy, vertical fin! If you're going to talk about airplanes, you always use the right names for things." Thus began my early training in aviation.

Soon, Bo was out of the biplane and assessing the damage. I closely followed every step he took and drank in his words as we circled the upside-down airplane. Half talking to himself and half explaining things to me, Bo kneeled to peer under and stretched to see over the damaged parts of his flying machine. Not once did he say anything like, "I sure did tear up that wingtip." Rather, the words that I heard were, "Now, here's what we're going to do, boy. We're going to find some good lumber and patch that spar." And, "We'll find a piece of thin pipe and make a new wingtip bow." And, "Now, you look here at this section of fabric. We'll patch that without even going into the aileron bay."

I was amazed that he didn't lament the fact that he had run out of gasoline or had failed to control his airplane. Presumably, he worked that out of his system during those few upside-down moments after the crash, when he pounded his fist on the instrument panel. He would not look back now. He only saw what was ahead. I sensed that this was a good man. His use of the word "we" to include me in his plans solidly riveted my desires to his.

As we continued to check each part of the airplane, I could see my father bumping his way across the pasture toward us in the Model T flat-bed truck.

"That's my father coming there," I warned.

"Well, maybe you ought to tell me his name, boy."

"His name is Peter, Peter Hawkins, but he goes by Pete."

"And I suppose you're Pete Hawkins Junior."

"No sir, my name's Samuel."

"Samuel? That's a good Bible name, just like Peter. Did your ma pick that name?"

"Yes, sir, she did. But it wasn't from the Bible."

"Oh? Where'd she get it then?"

"She had an Uncle Samuel on her mother's side that fought for Texas' Independence. She was real proud of him."

"You mean he fought at the Alamo?"

"No, sir. The Mexicans killed everybody at the Alamo. Uncle Sam lived to be 97. He was with Sam Houston at San Jacinto when they whipped the Mexicans."

"Well, boy, I'd be real proud to be named for a man like that."

My chest swelled with pride as my father stopped the truck beside the overturned airplane.

"Howdy," my father said as he stepped down from the tall truck.

"Howdy, sir," Bo replied.

"I'm Pete Hawkins," my father said, and extended his hand toward Bo.

"Please to meet you, Mr. Hawkins. I'm Bo Wages," replied Bo while shaking hands.

"You all right?" my father asked.

"Oh sure. That old airplane is strong enough to fly through a brick wall," Bo bragged.

There are few things as disastrous-looking as a damaged airplane lying on its back. My father ventured, "Well, maybe, but it looks like you got real trouble with it now."

"It's not as bad as it looks, sir. Why if I could find four or five good men, we could roll her back over on her wheels, and I could have her going again in nothing flat." Bo realized that he was an uninvited guest on someone else's land and tried to minimize the effort it would take to restore the biplane.

"Well, I've got a couple of Mexicans down in the barn milking, but them cows can't wait and this airplane can. They'll be done directly. You come on up to the house and have a cold drink," my dad concluded and motioned us toward the truck.

Riding on the back of the noisy flatbed, I couldn't hear what was being said. As I was watching intently through the small rear window, it was obvious that Bo was talking about flying because he occasionally waved his flattened hand through the air in graceful arcs. I strained to hear his story, but caught only fleeting words over the noise of the bumping truck.

Bump. Bump. "...airspeed was..." Bump. Rattle. "...back hard and..." Bump. As my father drove and quietly listened, Bo continued with more hand motions. Rumble rumble. "...rolled over and..." Bump. Rumble.

It was agonizing to be this close to a real aviator and not be able to hear his words. "Drive faster," I mumbled, hoping to reach our house before Bo's story was completely told.

Having seen us coming, my mother was waiting with three tall glasses of well water. The water was freshly pumped to be at its coolest. Taking one of the glasses, my father said, "Have a glass of water, Mr. Wages, and take a seat here in the shade."

Nothing was said for several minutes as the three of us enjoyed the still warmth of the summer afternoon and the sweet coolness of the water. My father was the first to speak. He broke the silence with his usual directness. "How long will it take you to fix it up?"

"Oh, don't you worry none, Mr. Hawkins. I'll have her out of your pasture before you know it," Bo answered defensively.

"That's not my worry. I've got a lot more pasture than I do cows. It's Sam here that I'm worried about. We depend on him to do as much around here as the next man. He just ran off and left a cow half milked when he heard you go over. He won't be worth a flip so long as you and that contraption are around here."

"Yes, sir, I understand," answered Bo while throwing me a knowing glance.

"So how long do you think it'll be?" my father pressed.

My father believed that a man should work the land, develop firm roots and, generation by generation, build the family strength. Bo could see that my father excelled in this belief. He also could see that his gypsy lifestyle stood in strong contrast. He realized that he could not escape my father's directness and answered almost apologetically, "Well, sir, to be perfectly honest, I don't have no money. I'll have to get a job somewhere and save up enough to buy the things needed to fix her up."

"A job? Haven't you heard about the Depression? There's a lot of good men standing in lines for jobs these days. Where would you get a job?"

"How about right here with you? You've got lots of machinery around this dairy and I'm real good with machinery."

"So am I," my father replied dryly, indicating his rejection of Bo's proposal.

"Yes, sir. I can see you are by the good looks of this place," Bo agreed. Then taking a different approach, Bo added, "But if I go somewhere else for work, I could only work on weekends and I would spend most of that time traveling. It could take a year to get her flying again. If I lived and worked here, I could work on her every night. I could have her going in a month or two."

I followed every word of the conversation, looking back and forth like a spectator at a tennis match. For a long moment my father and I studied each other while he weighed Bo's proposal. Finally he said, "Okay, Mr. Wages, you've got one month of room, board, and a dollar a day. We go to work at five A.M. and quit for supper after the evening milking. But there's one thing I want to make very clear. If either you or this boy start talking about airplanes or flying while there's work to be done, I'll load you and that airplane on my truck and dump you both on the other side of the county line."

Bo and I quickly agreed to my father's terms. Neither of us knew at the time that he had already planned to expand the size of the dairy herd and hire one more dairy hand.

With the cows milked and the evening sun nearing the horizon, my father and I, our two helpers, and the man who was to be my flight instructor were on our way to right the overturned biplane.

WAITING

YOU MIGHT THINK THAT A SUCCESSFUL CORPORATE pilot need only be a good pilot. Being able to fly well is important, of course, but equally important is being able to wait. The inability to wait patiently, not the inability to fly well, is what keeps some pilots from succeeding in this line of work.

Most of us can stand a little waiting, but extended waiting, hours of waiting with nothing to occupy the mind or body, is difficult. Typically, the average corporate pilot spends from four to six hours waiting for each hour flying. Some of this waiting can be agonizing, but there are good waits and bad waits, just as there are good flights and bad flights. One wait that stands out in my memory started with a sales demonstration of a 1979 Cessna 210 Centurion.

Normally, when the company I work for decides to change airplanes, the old airplanes are traded in for new ones. In this case, however, we were not going to replace the 210. We were selling it outright. The company had agreed to allow the prospective buyer to fly the airplane on his next business trip. However, our legal department had insisted that I, as the company's chief pilot, go along to protect the company's interests.

At first, I welcomed the flight because we were going to fly from Dallas to Sawyer, Texas. Being the county seat, Sawyer has an old courthouse. Texas is chock full of beautiful old courthouses, usually built on a square in the middle of town. Most of them were built between the Civil War and World War I. Courthouses of that period are very ornate. Some were built of colorfully shaded bricks and tiles. Some used native limestone; others used the rich red granite from central Texas. They all have high ceilings, beautiful woodwork, graceful stairways, as well as plenty of columns, towers, turrets, balconies, and all the extra frills that we now call *gingerbread*. Each building is uniquely different from all the others, and each has enough extra features sprinkled all over it to keep you gazing for longer than you'd realize.

Sawyer is a friendly little east Texas town filled with graceful older homes and small shops. Completely clothed in tall furry pine trees, the town relaxes to a sweet fragrance and an easy lifestyle. The airport, Adams Field, is a narrow slit cut out of those big pines; the thin gash in the forest can be spotted from miles away. The narrow 2,800-foot runway stretches between two small hills.

We were on a right downwind for landing to the north in the Centurion. Because there was no wind, we could have landed either way, but a north landing was chosen because there was no traffic and the terminal building was on the north end of the airport.

During our preflight inspection, I had learned some disturbing news from our prospective pilot. He had earned a private pilot's certificate and logged about 85 hours in an Ercoupe back in 1949. He hadn't flown since, but he had the money and a Centurion was what he wanted. He was in the left seat nervously jerking the controls and sweating. I was in the right seat doing a pretty good job of staying off the controls and acting nonchalant.

Well past our downwind key, he finally got the Centurion slowed to below gear and flap speed, and began to get all the stuff out for landing. Flying about half a day behind the airplane, he let the downwind become very extended. The airport was fading away behind my shoulder. He finally turned to base, turned again, and announced on a lo-o-o-ong final.

Actually, I didn't mind the long final. It gave me time to coach him through the landing checklist. It gave him time to get it all together and settle down. I explained that we'd go around if the rubber wasn't on the asphalt at the windsock.

"Approach at 80 knots," I advised. More sweat ran down his forehead as he struggled down to 90. To him, those woolly pines looked much too big and much too close. High, hot, and long we zoomed into the narrow gash in the forest that surrounded the runway.

Below the treetops, but a good 30 to 40 feet above the runway, there was nothing but hot, moist, dead air. The Centurion sank like a rock. "FLARE!" I yelled. The rubber screamed and smoked. The runway was vividly marked with parallel black lines, and the Centurion rebounded into the air. A little farther down we were on the runway again, and he applied the brakes hard. Fortunately, it's uphill both ways from the middle at Sawyer.

The only building on the airport is a small terminal building. It's just big enough to house restrooms and a small waiting room with a pool table. The airport was unattended and the pay telephone had been removed because of lack of use. Anxious to see the old courthouse again, I joined my passenger for the short walk to town. Coming upon the courthouse square, I recoiled in shock. The old courthouse was gone.

The good folks of Sawyer had been talked out of their beautiful old courthouse by some fast-talking architect selling the notions of economical construction and efficient air conditioning. The new one built in place of the old one was a simple, slab-sided, flat-topped box. More imagination goes into the boxes that a fancy pair of boots come in. Instead of standing for long periods to study the ornate designs and intricate workmanship, I could see the whole thing in one glance. Disgusted, I returned to the airport and the solitude of the country.

The first thing you notice about the country is the quiet. After your ears adjust from the buzzing and banging of the city to the quiet of the country, you can hear for miles. I listened to the barking of squirrels from somewhere deep in the piney woods. From another direction came a rustling splash repeated over and over; it could have been a raccoon washing his dinner. Faintly, from a great distance came the slow rhythmic chug-chug-chug of a single-cylinder steam-powered sawmill.

As I scanned my surroundings for the sources of these sounds, my eyes fell on the only airplanes at the airport. One was a dilapidated Aeronca Champ. It stood in weeds to its belly and the fabric was rotten. The other airplane was a Piper Cherokee 140 that looked reasonably airworthy and showed signs of occasional use.

I returned to the terminal building. I was already tired of waiting and anxious to go, but, like all corporate pilots, I was trapped. I was being paid to wait. I paced across the terminal's small waiting room, stopping only to carefully review an FAA bulletin issued in 1970 and a few magazines of similar date. Pacing was not the answer to my boredom, so I challenged myself to a game of pool; I decided to play rotation.

Rotation is the game in which you shoot at the balls in consecutive order, beginning with the number one ball. The missing eight ball didn't bother me because there was a spare cue ball that I could use in its place. This proved to be useful later in the game when the balls were scattered all over the table. Occasionally, I'd be working hard to urge some ball into a pocket (any ball into any pocket) and lose track of which cue ball was the eight ball. As a result, I could select the most favorably positioned cue ball as *the* cue ball. However, this new pool rule didn't help a bit. Pool is a lot like golf. You've got to hit the ball straight to do well, and I don't.

After walking about three miles around the pool table and sinking very few balls, my feet were hurting. There was nothing wrong with my feet. The socks I had hurriedly put on that morning had holes at the back of the heels. Running too late to change, I used the old Depression-days trick of pulling the socks down until the holes are under the heels. The excess sock is tucked under the toes and the shoe slipped on to hold it all in place. It was lumpy and crowded inside my shoes, so I decided against pool in favor of the big lounge chair beside the building's only window.

After a 15-minute argument, the chair and I had just about agreed on a comfortable position for a nap when some motion caught the corner of my eye. A chameleon was climbing up the wall. Chameleons and all sorts of other creatures abound in the lush greenery of east Texas. This one had done a fine job of matching his color to the brown color of the wall paneling. He was headed for a lofty perch on the curtain rod. After reaching his goal, he sat there admiring the inviting green bushes outside the window and turned a bright green. He sat there and worked up his courage to leap to a nearby branch, and that's just what he *tried* to do. The chameleon slammed into the window glass and fell to the floor.

In the terminal, there's a wine-colored carpet on the floor and that bright green chameleon looked awful and all out of place. He was on the floor recovering from his collision with the glass just long enough to take on a dark reddish hue.

When the chameleon felt a little better, he started up the wall toward the curtain rod and got all brown again. As before, the chameleon sat on the curtain rod until he was green and then took the same plunge with the same result. He was a determined rascal and kept trying, but each trip took longer than the one before, and he became more confused. After five cycles, the lizard began to trip his circuit breakers and was reaching the curtain rod with a red tail, brown body, and green feet. I decided to open the window so the chameleon wouldn't completely tumble his gyros and wind up behind the eight ball. I slipped the window open just as my passenger arrived for the return trip to Dallas. The waiting was over; it was time to fly again.

The Centurion roared down the runway. The Ercoupe pilot was wide-eyed, white-knuckled, and still behind the airplane as I coached him through the procedures. "Rotate at 75. Accelerate to 90. Toe brakes and gear up. Don't worry, we'll miss the trees. Manifold pressure back to 25. RPM back to 2,550. Flaps up. Speed to 110. Pitch trim. Cylinder head temp check. Oil temp check. All green. All go. Direct to Woodville VOR. Level at 6,500. Manifold pressure back to 23. RPM back to 2,400. Cowl flaps closed. Cylinder head temp check. Fuel pressure check. Pitch trim. Mixture set. EGT check. Rudder trim. Center the ball. Engine gauges. All green. All go."

Looking back, I could see Sawyer fading away behind us. I sure would like to have seen the smile on that lizard's face when he jumped off the curtain rod and went sailing through the open window, but the only thing I could make out was that ugly box they call a courthouse.

BO'S PLAN

BO WAGES' EMPLOYMENT ON OUR DAIRY INCLUDED room, board, and a dollar a day for one month. The "room" part of the deal turned out to be one of our little-used outbuildings. After it was emptied and cleaned, this shed became home and workshop for Bo. The "room" was not only acceptable, but became quite comfortable as things worked themselves down to routine. My school was in session again, and that meant classes until late afternoon and then homework, milking, and supper. The time between supper and bedtime belonged to Bo and me.

It had been necessary to disassemble the airplane to get it through the door of the shed. The fuselage dominated the center of the shed, while the wings hung on the wall waiting their turn for repair. Lacking the materials for repairs, we spent much of our time carefully studying the damaged areas and preparing them for repairs. From this careful piece-by-piece examination, and from Bo's explanations, I learned all of the bits and pieces that are collectively called an "airplane."

I first learned the major components; the wings, fuselage, powerplant, empennage, and landing gear were explained in detail. Then came a study of the controls. I learned of the ailerons, elevators, rudder, throttle, and trim tabs. Then on a more detailed level, Bo explained control cables, pulleys, bellcranks, pushrods, hingepoints, and control stops. Longerons, trusses, rosette welds, bungees, scarf joints, and other wondrous things became part of my working vocabulary. Bo and I discussed the importance of each piece, the way it was made, and its contribution to that magical event called "flight."

About half of the month given by my father had passed. We had gone as far as we could to prepare for the repairs. The parts and materials had been ordered from Houston, and they were to be delivered on the bus. As we entered the third week of Bo's month, the wait was becoming unbearable. We reluctantly accepted the fact that the repairs would not be completed within the time limit imposed by my father.

"What are we going to do?" I asked Bo.

"Well, boy, there ain't much we can do," came the matter-of-fact reply.

"Do you think my father will run you off at the end of your month?"

"You know your pa better than I do," Bo replied, tossing my question back to me.

"Well, I don't know what he's going to do. He ain't said much about it to me."

"How does your ma feel about it?"

"Aw, she don't never have anything to say about my father's business. All she ever says is 'Yes, Honey,' or 'Whatever you say, Honey,' when it comes to this dairy." After thinking about Bo's question a little more, I added, "The only thing I've heard her say was how you and Mrs. Cravens would make a nice couple."

"Mrs. Cravens. Who's Mrs. Cravens?"

"Her name's Lillian Cravens. She's a friend of my mother's. She's a widow now."

Bo had a blank, almost exhausted, look on his face and said, "I know that I look old and worn out beyond my years, boy, but that's no reason for your ma to try to match me up with some old widow woman."

"Mrs. Cravens ain't so old, Bo. She and my mother went to school together."

"Well, how come she's a widow then?" Bo quizzed.

"Mr. Cravens, her husband, he got killed about two years ago. He worked for the railroad in town and got squeezed between two boxcars. It was real sad because they had a closed-coffin funeral and nobody got to have a last look at him."

My description of Mr. Cravens' accident was wasted. Bo had not been listening. He was engrossed in some important thought. Then, "You know, boy, we just might have something here," Bo said as a sly look spread across his face.

"How's that?" I quickly asked.

"Well, there's one thing about your pa that's a fact. He's a hard-working man. That means he appreciates other men that work hard. So we've got to work so hard that we really impress him. Then, to cement the deal, we've got to get to know this Mrs. Cravens. It sounds to me like your ma is a matchmaker. If she thinks there's any chance in heaven that she could tie the knot between me and that widow, she wouldn't let your pa run me off for nothing. Between the hard work and the widow, I could probably stay here forever."

He paused and quietly considered the possibility of success. Nodding his head, he said, "Yep, that's what we have to do: work both ends against the middle. And I know it'll work." Slapping his thigh in affirmation, he added, "We're going to forget that airplane for a while and work like nobody ever has on this dairy. And then we've got to figure out a way to get your ma to introduce me to that widow woman without sounding like we're asking for it. You got any ideas?"

"Who, me?" I was surprised. "I wouldn't know how to go about a thing like that, Bo." The thought of trying to manipulate my mother into the introduction made me feel uneasy.

"Well, there ain't nothing to it, boy. Tomorrow night after I've got your pa all impressed with my hard work, we'll do it at the supper table. You and me will get to talking about how lonely it is to go traveling around this big old state, all the time not knowing where a man is going to lay his head at night. And I'll say good and loud, so's your ma can hear, how I might like to settle down and get some roots. That's bound to get me introduced to the widow woman."

"But what will I say to get it started?"

"Oh, don't worry, boy. Just play it by ear and it'll all come out fine. You just watch!"

I laid awake in bed late that night rehearsing, rejecting, and then re-rehearsing various lines that would have to sound spontaneous and natural at tomorrow's supper table.

I don't recall ever seeing a man work so hard and get so much done as Bo did the next day. In addition to the care, feeding, and milking of a dairy herd, there are a multitude of tasks to be completed on the dairy buildings, fencing, and equipment. Bo had literally rushed from one job to another between milkings and feedings. For thirteen hours he went like a runaway locomotive. If he continued working at that pace for the balance of the month given to him, there would be little for us to do for some time.

At the end of the day, we gathered in the washroom to clean up for supper. My father, usually talkative after a good work day, was strangely silent. As he washed from elbows down, I could see him occasionally look at Bo. He was impressed and confused by Bo's sudden and unusual vigor. As the washing neared an end, he said, "You really put in a day's work today, Bo."

Of all the things that Bo could have said, I have always thought that he said the very best thing to further impress my father. Tossing the towel to my father as he walked out of the room, he said, "A man can get to where he really likes this dairy business, Mr. Hawkins."

As my father dried his hands, he looked at me and said, "He might turn out to be a pretty good hand after all."

Knowing that this was just part of Bo's scheme, I could only muster a weak, "Yes, sir."

I usually approached the supper table with considerable eagerness, but tonight apprehension about the uncertain outcome of Bo's planned conversation clouded my appetite. According to our custom, my father took the first serving from each dish and then passed it to me on his left. The food then progressed single file around the table, stopping at my twin sisters, and finally reaching Bo. My mother, who always stood behind my father during the meal, would then relay each dish to the two Mexicans who sat at a table in the kitchen. (It didn't occur to me until I had almost reached manhood that she often ate a cold meal alone after we finished.) Tonight, however, her role would be more than an attentive wife and mother. Tonight, she would be drawn into Bo's scheme. My stomach clenched at the thought of it, and my appetite fell even further.

Father saw little of the girls during the day, so he often used most of our supper time to inquire about what they had been doing, how they were, and what he might do to help and counsel them. As the meal progressed through the usual small talk about the girls' day, my lack of interest in the food was noticed.

Father asked, "You feeling all right, Sam?"

"Yes, sir," I answered, trying to sound convincing and hoping that he wouldn't press the matter.

"There sure ain't nothing wrong with this food. You had better dig in," he said.

Seeing an excellent opening, Bo added, "That's right, Sam. This is great food. A fellow doesn't get food like this while traveling around."

There was my cue to pick up the conversation and lead Bo to his big line. My moment had come and I hung fire; I stared blankly at Bo. My mouth wouldn't work. Seeing that I was having difficulty, my father asked, "You sure you're all right, Sam?"

"Oh! Yes, sir," I jerked. My own words sounded strange and surprised me, but I found that I could talk again and quickly added, "I was just thinking about Bo traveling all around this big old state of Texas not knowing what he was going to get to eat at the next stop."

Aiming his comment at me more than Bo, father quickly added, "Yeah. That sure ain't much of a life."

Unknowingly, father had given Bo the perfect opening.

"You know, Mr. Hawkins, I'm inclined to agree with you. It sure ain't much of a life. I've been thinking a lot lately about finding a nice place like this to settle on and get some roots."

While all attention was drawn to Bo by his sudden confession, I stole a glance at mother through the corner of my eye. Although her expression had not changed, it seemed to me that her ears had raised up at least a full inch. She had taken the bait.

Seven Days
without Billy

A WEEK OFF AFTER A YEAR OF HARD FLYING ISN'T much. I was tired and the boss could see it. She said, "Take the King Air and go away with your family for a week." To get all the relaxation possible, I had returned to one of my favorite places: the beach. The airplane was safely tucked away in a hangar, and I intended to do absolutely nothing except let the sun and sea work their magic on my tired mind and muscles. Lying on the beach, I was warmed on one side by the pillowlike sand and on the other side by the brilliant sun. Relaxing halfway between sleep and awareness, my mind was completely void of thought.

As the veil of sleep lifted and fell, the sounds around me drifted in and out of my consciousness. Through the pleasant sounds of wind and wave came one sound that was out of place. My sleepy mind fumbled to fit this faint noise into the harmony of the beach, but couldn't. I tried to reject the offending vibrations as unreal or perhaps the beginning of a bad dream. The sound persisted, refused to be ignored, and grew stronger until the sweet web of sleep snapped and my eyes popped open. In the sky above me, a flame-red Citabria was noisily straining with the load of an aerial banner that advised me to use a certain suntan lotion.

At first, I was angered by this noisy intrusion into the quiet rest that I was enjoying, but as my eyes played along the banner a startling awareness came to me. That Citabria was pulling thirty-seven letters! I was amazed by this feat and reminded of the time that Billy Ford just managed to get one four-letter word into the air with a Stearman.

The old Stearman was worn out when Billy and I bought it from the Army Air Corps in 1946, and it didn't get a bit better during the year we flew it, even though we worked on it continuously. The brakes were particularly troublesome; as soon as the brake on one side was repaired, the brake on the other side would fail. I never flew that airplane with both brakes working at the same time. This led to the habit of landing with one wheel off the runway in tall grass or mud, so the good brake could be used.

The technique worked well except in a crosswind. The crosswinds always seemed to be on the wrong side for the brake that was working.

A more troublesome problem was trying to see around the radial engine. The number one cylinder sticks up along the centerline of the airplane, forcing a pilot to look around one side or the other. I usually leaned slightly to the left until the engine developed an oil leak on that side. Shortly after making a personal adjustment to the right side, the engine blew an exhaust gasket on that side. So the choice was then between looking left and seeing nothing but oil, or looking right and seeing nothing but fire.

The rest of the airplane was in a similar state of disrepair, so Billy and I agreed that we must do something to avoid a complete disaster. I suggested that we burn it, but with his usual optimism Billy suggested that we rebuild the Stearman to like-new standards. "But that would take a lot of money," I argued. With excitement flashing in his eyes, Billy explained that we were going to rig the Stearman for banner towing and make enough money to rebuild it.

I was thus reluctantly led into the banner-towing business by Billy Ford. I wasn't convinced that banner towing would work for us. For one thing, the Stearman was so weak that it couldn't pull the hat off your head without a strong tail wind. The engine compression was so low that, when parked into a wind, we had to tie the propeller down to keep it from windmilling. Furthermore, we had no banner letters and no banner-towing experience. It seemed hopeless to me.

The following morning, Billy came to the airport with a bulky bundle of brightly colored material rolled under his arm. With a boyish grin, obvious pride, and no small fanfare, Billy unrolled the bundle on the hangar floor. Stretched out before my unbelieving eyes, in a hand-stitched, quilt-like patchwork pattern, was a banner spelling out the word "FORD." A little embarrassed by his choice of words, Billy quickly explained that he selected that particular word because he was going to make the first flight and because "a little four-letter word like that won't overload our Stearman." And thus, all my doubts about this banner-towing business were put aside.

Billy had the Stearman lined up for takeoff. Oil was spraying out of its top and dripping out of its bottom. Fire spewed from the Stearman's leaky exhaust, and occasionally the engine would hit on all cylinders. That miserable old airplane looked desperate standing there knowing that it was about to be put to its ultimate test. But Billy was ready.

The banner was stretched out flat on the ground facing opposite the direction of takeoff and some 500 feet upwind from the Stearman. With a 500-foot rope attaching the banner to the airplane, the Stearman would have about 1,000 feet to take off and gather speed before picking up the load. If everything went according to Billy's plan, the banner would be briskly jerked into the air and would "fly" in the upright position. With terrible misgivings, I waved the signal that all was ready, and Billy opened the throttle wide.

The Stearman came down the runway spewing oil and flame, coughing and smoking. As Billy passed me at the banner, he had the Stearman's tail up, but the airplane was still below flying speed; all my questions would be answered in another 500 feet of runway. Billy coaxed the Stearman, laboring under its own weight, into the air with some slack left in the tow line. The line snapped taut and I could hear the Stearman groan; however, the instantaneous jerk that was supposed to yank the banner into the air just wasn't in that old airplane. The Stearman tugged as mightily as it could, shuddering near the stall, but the banner rushed away from my feet with insufficient speed to lift it into the upright position, or into the air.

Lying flat on its side, the multicolored banner skidded down the runway as Billy and the Stearman struggled for altitude and airspeed. While watching that desperate battle against gravity, I suddenly recalled the barbed wire fence at the end of the runway. A grim coldness gripped me as I visualized the banner entangled in the barbed wire and my friend being pulled to earth. Feeling helpless, but compelled by instinct, I started running toward the projected crash site. The banner continued to hug the runway until it hit a chuckhole that I had cursed many times during landings.

The sudden lurch imparted by the chuckhole caused the banner to suddenly erect itself; the word "FORD" was upright and readable, but the letters' bases still skidded along the runway. The fence was just ahead and sudden death seemed certain. My dash was spurred by the hope of somehow catching up to the banner and lifting it over the fence.

The banner entered a 100-foot grassy patch between the runway's end and the fence. Unmowed for some time, the tall wiry grass in this area grabbed and tugged at the banner. The tow rope was drawn extremely tight as the Stearman labored on. Then, suddenly, the banner was released by the grass, accelerated by the tightened rope, and catapulted inches above the fence. I was so astounded that I froze in my tracks to stare. The crisis seemed over, but the momentary speed and lift gained by the slingshot action of the tow rope was lost and the banner settled to the ground beyond the fence.

Our four-lettered word half bounced and half flew through the pastures beyond the airport, scattering chickens and cows alike. The farmers and ranchers south of the airport were not very friendly toward our flying as matters stood, but with this happening, I could see our troubles mounting. The banner went bounding along close to several houses; we were going to have some very upset people on our hands. The Stearman, however, was gradually winning its fight against gravity. The banner was flying more than it was bouncing. And then, after a time, there was no bouncing; Billy and that tired old Stearman had done it.

The banner was there for everyone to see—FORD—skimming along at rooftop level. Billy was so proud of himself and that old airplane that he buzzed back and forth across the town for nearly an hour. Each time he turned toward the airport, I would wave to him to land. He would cheerfully return my wave and turn back to buzz the community some more. When he finally had enough, he flew over the airport, dropped the rope and banner, then circled to land.

As I rushed out to get the banner off the runway, the sheriff drove out to my position. I had just gathered up the banner when he arrived. To him it must have looked like I was trying to hide behind an armful of guilt. The sheriff always chewed his cigar when he was mad. He gave me a no-nonsense look, took a couple of chews on his cigar, and explained that he had a lynch mob on his hands at the courthouse. He had calmed the complaining crowd by promising to bring the pilot before the judge right away.

I felt much like the sheriff; I could have broken Billy's neck. Instead I made a sheepish attempt to explain the whole thing away as something unfortunate, unavoidable, and never to be tried again. The sheriff's chewing indicated that he wasn't impressed.

Billy had the Stearman on the ground and taxied toward us; I was so happy to see my friend alive after his narrow escape from death that I momentarily put aside our problem with the sheriff.

As Billy climbed out of the Stearman, I rushed over to shake his hand, but not for a job well done. We had just completed the worst job of banner towing in aviation history. I shook his hand, just happy he was alive. As I pumped gleefully on Billy's right hand, the sheriff snapped his handcuffs on Billy's left hand and said: "Come on son, let's go see the judge. You've been enough trouble for one day."

The "due process" that followed was more like an inquest than a trial. There was no one to speak for Billy but himself, and each time he tried to talk the crowd would shout him down. I wasn't going to help him because the joy of having him alive instead of entangled in the wreckage of the Stearman had worn off; I was just as mad as some of the town folk.

There was a good deal of shouting, fist-waving, and foot-stomping by everyone, until the judge pounded for silence with his gavel. When we were quiet, the judge looked sternly at Billy, and said: "Son, I find you guilty of everything you've been charged with and maybe a few things we don't know about yet. You're sentenced to three days in the county jail."

The judge was a good man, but I felt that the sentence handed down was out of line. I leaned over to confer with the sheriff, and we quickly agreed that the sentence was not proper. We requested a conference with the judge and after a few minutes of careful exaggeration and friendly coaxing, we were able to get the judge to make the sentence "seven days in the county jail," which suited me and everyone else a lot better.

Although more than 35 years had slipped away, I felt good stretched out on the beach thinking of Billy Ford stretched out in that jail. In fact, if this week proved to be as peaceful and quiet as the week that Billy was in jail, I would go back to work a very rested man.

While that thought played in my mind, the Citabria pulling the 37-lettered suntan lotion banner puttered off into the silent distance, and I dozed off to the music of the beach.

UNEXPECTED
HELP

MY FATHER HAD GIVEN BO WAGES ONE MONTH TO get his wrecked biplane repaired and off the dairy, but the materials and parts necessary to complete the repairs had not yet arrived from Houston. We helplessly watched as the precious few days remaining quickly disappeared. Now, there were only five days left in Bo's month.

As the deadline approached, it occupied more and more of my concern. Should Bo have to leave before the repairs were completed, I would lose my chance to fly. This disappointment loomed large for me and popped in and out of our conversations with increasing regularity. I clung to the hope that my father would somehow forget the date, while Bo had confidence in his plan to use my mother's matchmaking instincts. "Don't forget your ma and Mrs. Cravens," he had said.

"Bo, my mother don't have anything to do with it. My father runs this dairy and everything connected with it," I said.

"Not so, boy, not so. You don't ever see it or ever hear it, but I can tell you that your ma is a strong woman. She helps control things in her own quiet way. You just wait and see," he had challenged.

In spite of Bo's reassurances, I felt that his plan was not going to work. Our first indication came on Saturday night at the supper table, where the plan had been put into motion days earlier. Mother was usually quiet while standing behind father during the meal. She wanted only to be of help and had little to add to our conversations. We were all surprised when, after everyone had been served, she quietly said: "Mr. Wages, I have a message for you."

It was so unusual to hear her speak at the supper table that everyone stopped in mid-bite. There wasn't the least clatter of a fork or ruffle of a napkin as all faces turned toward her. "The mailman stopped in today. He said that Mr. Mullins at the bus station has a package from Houston for you."

"The parts, Bo! The parts are here!" I eagerly told Bo what everyone at the table had already figured out.

"Well, thank you, ma'am. I'm real pleased to hear that, but you know better than most that milking cows is a seven-day-a-week job. I don't know how I would ever get to town. Do you think that mailman would bring the package out here?" Bo replied.

"I don't think that will be necessary, Mr. Wages. I have a friend who is coming to visit tomorrow after church. She can bring it to you." mother said.

I was trying to figure out who was the slickest. Was it Bo for cooking up this scheme, or was it my mother for bringing Lillian Cravens and Bo together with the much-awaited parts?

Sunday arrived and I rocked restlessly on the hard wooden church bench. As the ladies pumped their seashell-shaped fans near their faces and the preacher went sleepily through his sermon, I dreamed of soaring effortlessly through cloud-filled skies, of rolling, spinning and stalling through the vast blue, and of the complete freedom and unending joy of flight. My spell was broken by the final "Amen" as the service was over. We could resume rebuilding the biplane.

The rebuilding would officially begin with the arrival of the parts being delivered by Mrs. Cravens. She still had the 1929 Model A sedan that Mr. Cravens had bought shortly before the Depression set in. As we waited and watched for the sedan, we looked frequently up the road she would travel from town to our front door. As we waited, it came to me that everyone was outdoing themselves. My sisters were still in their frilly Sunday dresses and white patent-leather shoes. They were dashing between the hallway mirror and one of us to ask some silly question: "Are my curls straight in the back? When I curtsey, should I keep my hand out to the side or lift the hem of my dress like this?"

"How should I know? Go ask Mom," I said.

Mother and Juanita, our maid, were having a regular footrace around the kitchen and dining room. Although their meals were always something special, they were extending themselves today. This meal was taking on the proportions and variety of a feast.

Bo, father, and I looked like clothing-store dummies. We were still in our buttoned-up Sunday best. Since coming home from church we had washed our faces, polished our shoes, cleaned our fingernails, and slicked down our hair again.

Bo paced rigidly about the living room. He had been wedded only to airplanes and flying since the early days of World War I. From his late-evening tales of gun duels in the skies over entrenched troops in France, I knew that he was a man of skill and courage. I knew that he could have met any enemy pilot in a duel to the death with calm determination. Meeting the gentle Lillian Cravens in our living room was another matter; however, with sweaty palms and dry lips, he was visibly tense and worried. Each time he passed me in his nervous pacing, he would say: "What'll I talk about? She probably don't know nothing about airplanes and I don't know nothing else."

Father was his usual restless self when visitors were coming. Barking orders at everyone, he absolutely insisted that everything be clean and orderly; neatness was his passion. Not one flowerpot could be out of place on the front porch. Each and every fallen leaf had to be raked and disposed of. He had the two Mexicans in a frenzy of activity grooming the yard and house.

I was the only one that had a cool head and kept everything in clear focus. I wanted those airplane parts.

"Here she comes!" cried my sister in a high-pitched squeal. My mother made one last dash around the dinner table, checking the placement of each fork and napkin. My father ran to the porch waving his arms and shouting instructions in Spanish: "Get the brooms and rakes back behind the house." Mother was stripping the apron from her front and shooing Juanita off to the kitchen. My sisters were grooming each other and practicing their curtseys. Bo was gripped by fear and turning pale. I was itching to grab the parts and rush off to the biplane.

Somehow, each of us regained enough composure to find our way out of the house and form into a group at the edge of the driveway as Mrs. Cravens pulled in. Although she had visited several times since her husband's death, only recently had I come to realize that she possessed a rare and quiet beauty. Tall, thin, and discreetly shapely, she seemed to glide out of the car with effortless rhythm. Her flowing hair and clear complexion were balanced by full moist lips that complemented her straight white teeth. She could disarm a demon with her warm and friendly smile.

She always greeted mother first. As she handed mother a covered dish as her contribution to the meal, they hugged and kissed each other on the cheek. Then, with my mother, she would greet the rest of the family. To my sisters, she said: "My, you two are growing into beautiful young ladies. Next thing you know, all the boys in town will be out here on your doorstep." The girls giggled and blushed.

"Here's a little something that every young lady should have," she said, while handing each girl a small box. Inside the boxes they found thin gold necklaces. The girls jumped and squealed. Mrs. Cravens then turned to my father, took his hand, and said: "Pete, I just can't get over your place. The whole dairy looks like a picture postcard. It's just gorgeous. It makes me feel so good and so welcome."

It was always my turn next. Taking my hands she said: "Sammieee." She drug it out a lot longer than I would have liked. It had never bothered me before, but I was trying to be a little bigger and a little older in Bo's eyes. I felt embarrassed by her greeting. "How are you?" she continued.

"I'm fine, ma'am."

"You're growing into a fine man, Sam. Here's something for you to wear to church."

Folded neatly in white paper was a necktie similar to the one she had made for my father last Christmas.

"Thank you, ma'am."

"You get your Daddy to show you how to tie it, Sam."

Arm-in-arm with my mother, she moved finally to Bo. He was standing so close to me that it looked like he was trying to hide. I could feel him tremble.

"Lillian, this is Bo Wages. Bo, this is Lillian Cravens," my mother said to the two with a look of accomplishment.

Mrs. Cravens extended her hand toward Bo. It was a soft hand that was a pleasure to hold, but Bo failed to respond. I glanced at Bo. Already tense and nervous, he became mortified when confronted with the beauty and grace of Lillian Cravens. He stood there as stiff as an ax handle and as speechless as a stump. I eased my foot over and kicked him on the ankle. He jerked to life like a robot and rigidly pumped her hand up and down. The only words that he could muster were, "Pleased, ma'am. Pleased."

"You're the man with the airplane, aren't you?"

Relaxing slightly at the sound of the word "airplane," Bo responded, "Why, yes, ma'am."

"Well, I would dearly love to see it. Do you think you could show it to me after dinner?"

Her unexpected interest in the airplane brought new life to Bo. His color slowly returned to normal. He even smiled as he answered, "I'd be happy to, ma'am."

She smiled a thank you at Bo. Then, arm-in-arm, mother and Mrs. Cravens led the rest of us toward the house and our waiting meal.

Mother had craftily rearranged the dining table seating. The girls' chairs had been shifted so that Mrs. Cravens would be seated next to Bo. After the prayer had been said and our plates served, everyone fell into an awkward silence; each person politely waited for another to begin a conversation. My usually quiet mother again surprised us by saying, "Lillian, Mr. Wages flew airplanes during the war and has even been to France."

Surprised and impressed, Mrs. Cravens turned to Bo and said, "You don't say?"

Bo mustered a shy, "Yes, ma'am."

Mrs. Cravens placed her hand on Bo's arm and said, "Tell me what it's like, Bo."

Bo broke the final barriers of shyness when he asked, "Do you mean what it's like to fly, or go to war, or to go to France?"

With a delightful laugh, Mrs. Cravens said, "Why, you silly man, I mean all of it."

Bo responded with what he knew best and began a description of flight; from that point on, I never saw anything like it. Those two sat there through the whole meal and talked about nothing but airplanes and flying. Bo would no sooner finish one flying tale than Mrs. Cravens would ask a question that would lead him to another story. She was sincerely interested and that fired Bo's imagination. He entertained us for more than an hour with his wild tales and vivid descriptions of aerial combat. By the time dinner was nearing an end, he and Mrs. Cravens were like old friends who had met after a long absence.

The meal wound down and the conversation drifted to the biplane. Over a large piece of lemon meringue pie, Bo described the repairs necessary to make it fly again. Mrs. Cravens surprised him by asking, "When it's all fixed up, Bo, will you take me for a ride?"

I thought Bo was going to loop-the-loop right there in the dining room. I was soaring with him and blurted, "Why don't we get the parts out of the car and go work on it right now?"

My father coughed heavily and brought us back to earth. "After the evening milking, Sam."

After the meal, which lasted until almost three P.M., the women busied themselves with washing dishes and putting things away, and the men returned to the dairy. When the milking and chores were completed, Bo and I spent another hour with Mrs. Cravens. We moved the large package of parts from her car to the barn, showed her the biplane, and talked more about flying.

The mid-September sun was touching the distant horizon when Mrs. Cravens said, "Bo, I'm thrilled with your airplane and look forward to my ride, but for now, I must be going."

Bo's soaring mind and spirit became strangely serious as he asked, "Will you be coming to visit again?"

"Why, yes, Bo," she replied, with a warm smile. "I want to see the airplane go back together so I can learn more about it."

"We should have the wingtip ready for cover by Wednesday night. Would you like to come and watch?"

"No," she said. Bo's smile crashed around his chin and his spirits spiraled earthward like his powerless biplane had. Then with a smile she continued, "I have no intention of watching. I want to help."

Bo soared through another loop.

The surprise of having Mrs. Cravens interested enough to want to help repair the biplane spurred Bo into incessant activity. He continued his vigorous and productive work about the dairy during the day, and then pressed me and himself relentlessly in repairing the biplane at night. We had encountered the expected delay while making the scarf joint in the broken wing spar. We were terribly impatient with it, but you simply cannot hurry a glue joint. We had worked well past midnight each night since the parts had arrived. Bo now insisted on even longer hours, explaining, "We've got to have this wingtip ready for cover when Mrs. Cravens gets here tomorrow night."

The great urgency that Bo expressed could have been of no importance, but this particular day marked the end of the month given him by my father. The cows had been milked, fed, and bedded down for the night. We were at the supper table and the food had made its single-file progression around the table. As we all ate, father asked, "How are you doing on the airplane, Bo?" It wasn't a polite question expressing interest. It was a demand for a progress report.

"It's coming along just fine, Mr. Hawkins. We put the final touches on the woodwork last night. If we can get the wingtip bow made and installed this evening, we'll be ready for covering tomorrow night."

"You two have been working some long hours out there." my father probed.

"Yes, sir. We're working to get it ready for cover by tomorrow night when Mrs. Cravens comes," Bo explained.

"That's all well and good for you and Lillian, but I'm concerned that this boy won't stand up to those hours. You've got to remember that his first job is his school work. His chores around here come next. Fixing your airplane comes last. We can't let that interfere with things that are more important."

"Yes, sir," Bo answered.

I didn't feel that Bo's response adequately satisfied my father's misgivings and that he might restrict my hours. I quickly added, "Those hours ain't too long for me. I'm doing just fine in school and with all my chores." Actually, I had fallen asleep once or twice in history class.

Bo further reassured my father. "If we can get the wingtip bow on tonight, we'll be through with these long hours. It's just that I promised Mrs. Cravens."

There was a slight smirk on father's face as he said, "Yes, I know she wants to help. Can't understand why, but I know she does."

"She'll be a big help, Mr. Hawkins. Women are good at stretching and stitching airplane fabric. It's real good material and they seem to enjoy working with it."

"Well, even if you finish the wingtip tomorrow night, won't that leave a lot to be done?" Father probed.

"It'll leave the vertical fin and rudder." Bo answered, trying to make the job seem smaller than it was.

"Then the whole airplane has to be put back together, right?" My father knew the correct size of the job.

"That's right, Mr. Hawkins," Bo cautiously answered.

"And then it has to be tested and adjusted, right?" Father pressed.

"Yes, sir," Bo answered with less self-assurance.

"And that could take weeks, right?"

Apprehensively, Bo answered, "It could."

"I don't know if you remember or not, but today marks a month since you crashed that machine in my pasture."

Bo and I grew solemn and quiet. Our eyes were fastened tightly on my father. We feared that he was about to bring an end to Bo's employment and to my dream of flying. "You realize, of course, that I was being generous in giving you work for a month," father said, and then paused as if waiting for agreement by Bo.

The pause continued for much too long. Suddenly realizing that my father wanted agreement, Bo jerked, "Oh, yes, sir, and I'll always be indebted. You can rest assured that I'll get the airplane finished in a month just like I said—counting from the day I got the parts." Bo was gambling on a new definition of the month.

My father quickly scuttled that notion. "Don't you try to stretch it on me, Bo. A month's a month! I have to count my expenses from the day I hired you," my father grumped.

"Well, sir, there wasn't much I could do before the parts came."

"Yes, I know, but I'm a businessman. Basically, I'm paying you room, board, and a dollar a day to fix up your airplane."

Bo quickly defended his position. "In a way, that's right, and in a way, it ain't. Having me here has allowed you to expand the size of your herd. And you're getting ten to twelve hours of hard work each day and every day."

"Well, I have for the past week or so, but until then, you couldn't call what you were doing *work*."

Ever the gambler, Bo ventured, "I was just learning this dairy business. Now that I know what to do and how to do it, I like tending them cows. I was hoping that you might keep me on and even give me a raise."

The mention of a raise caused my father to choke on a bite of food. He coughed into his napkin as his face reddened. I had seen this red before. It wasn't from choking. It always preceded a burst of anger. He slammed his napkin to the table and said, "Now you listen here, Mr. Bo Wages. You can take that contraption you call an airplane and..." His words abruptly ended as my mother placed her hand on his shoulder.

Still glaring at Bo, his nostrils flared, but he had nothing else to say. As my mother patted his shoulder, he relaxed and returned to his meal. After chewing several bites slowly, he continued, "A raise? Now that's another question. I'm trying to decide if I should keep you on or let you go—not if I should give you a raise."

"Maybe a raise is too much to ask, but I'd hate to move on now, Mr. Hawkins. I like this part of Texas and plan to put down some roots hereabouts."

"Well, Bo, I'll tell you what...," father was trying to restrain the last remnants of his quick anger and to make striking a bargain with Bo sound like he was making a concession. "I won't give you a raise, but if you continue working as hard as you have the last week, I can keep you on for another month."

"I appreciate that, sir, and I'll take it," Bo answered.

As Bo accepted my father's conditions for continued employment, I noticed that my mother had again placed her hand on my father's shoulder and gently patted her approval. It was clear that the decision to keep Bo on the dairy had been made earlier by my parents. Father only needed reminding during his moment of anger. Bo's plan had worked, and I learned that my mother's influence was far greater than I had ever thought.

FRANKLIN'S BIG EVENT

IF YOU SHOULD EVER BE NEAR MAYPEARL, TEXAS, STOP and ask an old-timer, "Isn't this the town where Bonnie and Clyde held up the bank?" In all likelihood, you will be treated to a vivid and somewhat boastful description of the bank at Maypearl, and a shot-by-shot narrative of the robbery. People of an area remember a significant event like that, and pass the tale along from generation to generation.

I was thinking of this as I leveled the Beechcraft King Air at 11,500 feet on a run from Abilene to San Antonio. Generally, I'm on an IFR flight plan and stick to the airways, but I was solo on this beautifully clear day and decided to shun the maps and mikes and go direct. I wasn't concerned about straying off course because I had made this particular run many times during the Civilian Pilot Training Program.

The CPT, as it came to be called, came along at the tail end of the Depression and lasted through the early days of World War

II. I satisfied the commercial pilot cross-country requirements by ferrying run-out school aircraft from the CPT base at Abilene to the overhaul depot at San Antonio. I had crisscrossed this part of Texas many times. Each time, as now, this course took me over the peaceful little town of Franklin, Texas. Like Maypearl, Franklin had its big event that people remember and talk about.

Franklin's remembered event started with one of those ferry flights. I was flying a ragged old Fleet that was used for primary training. Taylor Biggs was flying a Meyers OTW used for advanced training. There wasn't anything seriously wrong with the Fleet; it was just worn out. The Meyers, however, was a different story. Outwardly, it appeared to be in excellent condition, but while it was in the shop for an oil change, a routine inspection revealed large quantities of metal in the oil screen.

All work stopped on the Meyers because CPT policy required that any aircraft showing signs of engine failure must be returned to the depot in San Antonio. While the plane awaited a ferry flight to the depot, many of the instruments were exchanged for inoperative instruments. Other bits and pieces just disappeared. The Meyers was riskier than the Fleet and I was concerned that Taylor had been assigned as the pilot. He only had about forty hours flying time and had been given only a brief checkout in the Meyers.

Taylor was young, frisky, and eager to demonstrate the performance advantage of the Meyers over the Fleet. About thirty minutes out of Abilene, we were out of sight of anyone connected with the home base, and Taylor went wild.

He began barrel-rolling the Meyers around the Fleet and having a good time. He would fly below me and then inverted above me as he rolled both left and right. After tiring of the barrel rolls, he started looping. He would charge ahead, enter a loop, soar high above me, and try to time his recovery to come out alongside the Fleet. I concerned myself with maintaining separation and keeping us pointed in the general direction of San Antonio.

The aerial horseplay went on for a lot longer than I liked, but Taylor finally had enough and settled down for the long grind. I was particularly happy about his return to straight and level flight because power for aerobatics only stressed the engine more. It had already served notice that all was not well within.

My happiness was short-lived. Whatever had deposited the metal particles in the oil screen suddenly let go with a sharp bang. Oil flew out of the engine, covering the airplane. The prop froze in the vertical position, and Taylor Biggs was on his way to his first forced landing.

From my vantage point above him, I could see that he had decided to land on the state highway below us. This wasn't a bad choice, *except* for the way things turned out. He began a series of spiraling turns to lose altitude, bring the airplane into the wind, and line up with the highway. On that day, the wind was right down the highway, but we were very close to the tiny town of Franklin. This wouldn't normally present a serious problem, but Taylor was an inexperienced pilot and totally unfamiliar with the gliding characteristics of the Meyers, especially with an engine out.

Without power, the Meyers was sinking fast. I found myself spiraling down with the stricken airplane and shouting, "Roll out, Tay! Roll out! Save your altitude! Go beyond the town!" He entered another turn and found himself too low to land beyond Franklin. Taylor had committed himself to a choice between selecting a secondary (and crosswind) landing site or landing on the highway, toward the town. One axiom handed student pilots is to not make a last-minute change in the choice of an emergency landing site, and he didn't. He was headed straight up the highway for Franklin, Texas.

Many small Texas towns are built around a central square. The square provides a location for a courthouse or park surrounded by the town's businesses. Franklin wasn't that big, though. Franklin grew up around the intersection of two paved highways: one was the state highway that Taylor had selected for his landing; the other was a farm-to-market road. On the corners of the intersection rest the most prominent buildings in Franklin: a grocery store, a filling station, a fire station, and a church. Spread out around these buildings, and along the four legs of the intersection, were the other businesses and homes of the 300 or so people who lived in Franklin.

Taylor had about 1,500 feet of highway between himself and Franklin. That should have been enough to get a Meyers down and stopped, but this Meyers had no brakes, an inoperative airspeed indicator, and an oil-smeared windshield. Without good vision and an airspeed indicator, Taylor had allowed the airspeed to build during his spiraling descent. This excess speed and the rising heat from the highway buoyed the Meyers up, and it went sailing right into Franklin.

Taylor had the mains on the highway as he passed the first

few houses. Still following behind, I was shouting, "Ground-loop it, Tay! Ground-loop it!" Without brakes, Taylor and the Meyers rolled straight ahead. The situation was bad now, but with a little luck he just might roll in one side of Franklin and out the other.

Early in this business of flying, we learn not to depend on luck because it can work both ways. At Franklin that day, it went against Taylor Biggs. Some farmer had angle-parked his wagon in front of the grocery store. The horse and wagon cut off about one-third of the already too-narrow highway. Taylor's right wing ripped into the wagon. The Meyers spun through the intersection and came to rest on its nose in front of the filling station. The frightened horse bolted straight ahead into the grocery store. From my position overhead, I could see that no one was hurt, but excitement gripped Franklin.

Only a few people in Franklin had ever seen an airplane first-hand, and no one was going to miss this event. The whole town turned out. Everyone was shouting with excitement and maneuvering for a better look. The kids were all over the place. A group of men rolled the fire truck out of the station and began dousing Taylor and the Meyers. I decided to land, and it was a good thing that I did because the excitement had only just begun.

I had the Fleet parked along the highway and was running into town, not knowing that a truckload of heavy crude oil was eastbound on the state highway. At the same time, a truckload of chickens was northbound on the farm-to-market road. Both trucks would pass through Franklin. During those times of Depression, truck drivers were accustomed to having the highways to themselves. Generally, they would blow their horn at the edge of a small town like Franklin as a warning that they were coming through. Seldom would they let up on the accelerator.

True to form, and unseen by each other, the two truck drivers blew their horns in unison. The people of Franklin dutifully stepped out of the intersection, and the stage was set. Perhaps it was the sight of all the people, or perhaps it was the surprise of seeing an airplane standing on its nose in front of the filling station, or per-haps it was just due to happen, but neither driver looked for the other nor let up on the gas. They met at the center of the intersection. There was a tremendous crash, and the whole thing was witnessed by the entire population of Franklin.

Both trucks came to rest in the fire station driveway, opposite the filling station and damaged Meyers. The two drivers had climbed from the trucks and were shouting and shoving at each other over who had the right of way. The impact of the collision ruptured the tank containing the oil, and thousands of gallons of heavy black crude flooded the intersection. The chicken truck had overturned and 300 or 400 chickens were on the loose—slogging their way to freedom through a knee-deep (on a chicken) sea of blackness.

From somewhere in the memory of these Depression-weary west Texas folks, they recalled a promise: "a chicken for every pot." They all started grabbing for the chickens. At first they stretched neatly and used tidy little grabs from the edge of that black sea of oil, but as the chickens flapped in their desperate attempt to escape, everyone was coated with a spray of blackness. Soon, all the people of Franklin were slipping, sliding, falling, and crawling after a chicken in the middle of the intersection. The dogs came from all around and added to the frenzy by barking at the already hysterical chickens. The kids were running, shouting, and enjoying the whole thing immensely.

The firemen couldn't decide if they should douse the Meyers or squirt the oil truck, so they were spraying aimlessly at everything. As the situation was obviously out of control, I leaned toward Taylor and said, "Tay, when these people sober up, we just might wind up in jail. Let's get out of here." And we did. Unnoticed by the frantic folks of Franklin, we made a well-timed retreat to Abilene in the Fleet.

I don't know just how long that melee continued (I've heard conflicting reports over the years), but three days later a recovery crew from Abilene went down to load the Meyers on a trailer and reported seeing "quite a lot of oil and chicken feathers."

Today, if you ask an old-timer near the town of Franklin, "Isn't this the town where an airplane crashed some years back?" you will be told of Franklin and The Big Crash. You might be told how the mayor sprained his ankle or how the preacher's wife pulled her hamstring, but whatever you are told, it will be told with all of the zest and pride that the people of Maypearl have when describing Bonnie and Clyde's bank robbery.

TEXAS WIND

IN ORDER TO HASTEN THE REMOVAL OF THE BIPLANE
from his property, my father extended Bo's employment on our
dairy. Bo was to continue his hard work during the day, and
repair the biplane at night. Bo was happy with this arrangement,
and assured me that we would be flying soon. He was going to
give me flying lessons in exchange for my help. I felt that this was
the best gift that he, or my father, could give me, and I was thrilled
at the prospect of soon being able to fly.

Work on the spar and wingtip bow was complete. We were
ready for the fabric covering on Wednesday night as planned. Mrs.
Cravens arrived shortly after we had finished supper. Although
father had been his usual self, barking orders at everyone about
cleanliness and order, Mrs. Cravens didn't even go into the house.
During our driveway greeting, Mrs. Cravens said to mother, "If
you will excuse me, Mary Jane, I think I'll join the boys at the
airplane."

"Lillian Cravens!" mother funned, "You're as bad as Sam
when it comes to that airplane."

Unashamed of her interest, Mrs. Cravens answered, "Yes, I am. It's exciting!"

"Well, I hope the weather doesn't get any worse while you're out there in that old barn," mother said.

An early evening overcast had rolled in ahead of a brisk southeast wind. At this point, father joined the conversation, saying, "Just between us, I wouldn't mind if it started raining right now and rained all night. In case you haven't noticed, we're in the middle of a drought. We need the moisture a lot more than we need that airplane."

"Oh, Pete," mother scolded.

With that, Bo, Mrs. Cravens, and I went to the barn and started fitting the fabric to the wingtip. As the wind whistled and moaned around the eaves of the barn, Mrs. Cravens commented, "My, the wind does blow at times. Just listen."

Bo eagerly picked up her comment and said, "Now, you being from west Texas and all, you should be accustomed to the wind blowing."

Fondly remembering her youth with a pleasant smile, Mrs. Cravens said, "Yes, I remember how hard it would blow out there."

Bo pushed the conversation ahead as we began stretching the fabric to the wingtip bow. "There may be places in the world where it sometimes blows harder, but for day in and day out blowing, there ain't no wind like the wind in west Texas. There have been a thousand stories told about how hard Texas wind blows, and there will be a thousand more. But, the whole story won't ever get told because most of the storytellers don't know the real secret of Texas wind."

"What on earth are you talking about?" Mrs. Cravens asked.

"Well, ma'am, I'll tell you the secret about our wind here in Texas."

He looked carefully to the left and then to the right, suggesting that he wanted no ears but ours to hear his words. He leaned closer to us and motioned us to move closer. We leaned forward to meet his whispered words.

"There ain't more than a few breaths of air that have ever left the state of Texas since the Maker set the earth to spinning."

Mrs. Cravens sat up straight and said, with a half laugh, "Now, Bo...." She was cut off by Bo.

"Don't laugh, Ma'am. There's more to this than shows on first think. It's always going to blow one way or the other in Texas because the air enjoys rushing from one corner of the state to another."

"What do you mean by that, Bo?" she asked, while stretching a small section of fabric around the wingtip bow. I sensed that another of his tales was emerging, and I waited eagerly for his answer.

"The wind likes it here in Texas. It's got a good deal and knows it. It can whistle through the tall pine trees of east Texas, or it can howl through the canyons of the Big Bend. It can rumble across the choppy Hill Country, or it can zephyr across the Panhandle Plains. There are hundreds of interesting places for the wind to twist and turn, and ripple and zip."

Bo reached over the wing to help hold the fabric taut while Mrs. Cravens stitched another seam.

"Now for instance, say there's a big pile of air setting right in the middle of Texas basking in the sun. All that sounds pretty good, but soon the air gets too hot because the Texas sun can really bear down. Well, about the time that air gets good and hot, it spies all that cool water setting down there in the Gulf of Texas...."

I interrupted and corrected Bo. "You mean the Gulf of Mexico, Bo."

"Listen, boy, you can call it whatever you like, but I never did see any reason to give our Gulf to the Mexicans. Now, as I was saying, the air gets good and hot and spies all that cool water down there in the Gulf of Texas and, SWOOOSH, it stampedes offshore to dabble its toes and cool its heels."

Just a hint of laughter crossed Mrs. Craven's face as she glanced at me. I shared her pleasure with a small smile as we turned our attention back to the fabric and to Bo. He pointed out several new areas of fabric to be stretched and stitched and said, "Well, while the air sets there enjoying the coolness of the water, two things are happening: the air's getting wetter and heavier. It sets there and soaks, and cools, and gets heavier and heavier. It gets so heavy that the lower layers are squeezed by the heavy upper layers, like the poor kid at the bottom of a pile-on. And directly, the bottom is squeezed so hard that it comes squirting out like a wet watermelon seed. It rushes back on shore in a gale. It goes whistling back across the state carrying along all sorts of clouds and rain."

Mrs. Cravens tied the last knot in the stitching and the wingtip was covered. The next step was to apply the dope that would seal and tighten the fabric.

Bo opened the can of dope and continued his story as the barn filled with the stimulating aroma of nitrate dope. "Sometimes that air gets up enough speed to cross the whole state as it spreads clouds and rain. But, as the first onrushing wave hits the Red River, it comes to a screeching halt. It's the sight of Oklahoma that does it. Meanwhile, there's plenty of air still charging northward from the Gulf. Now, you can plainly see what's going to happen. With the air in front stopped and the air behind charging hard, it begins to pile up all along the border until there's a pile a thousand miles high."

While I held the can of dope, Mrs. Cravens smoothly applied brushstroke after brushstroke under Bo's watchful eye. He leaned close to the wing, squinted with one eye, and pointed out small areas not fully covered with dope as he continued.

"Well, from way up on the top of that pile, the air can see all the way to Canada—across the whole middle of the U.S. And it sees a million miles of nothing but flat, and more flat—which ain't very interesting to some devilish air looking for a place to play. Looking to the northwest, it sees the Rocky Mountains. Why them things ain't nothing but uphill all the way and that ain't no fun either. So it looks back over its shoulder and sees all the good places in Texas to play."

"Now, any fool can see what's about to happen. The upper layers of that pile, being stretched out almost to the moon, have gotten so cold that the air has turned an icy blue color. Frozen stiff, it comes tumbling down off the top of that pile headed back toward Texas. By the time it gets to the bottom of that mountain of air, it's rolling like a runaway freight train. That frozen blue mass roars by people and places so fast that folks drinking from a fountain often get hit in the face with icicles as it goes by."

By this time Mrs. Cravens was chuckling so that I had to take over the brushing. Bo held the dope can, and in all seriousness said, "Now if you was frozen as stiff as a tombstone and had sharp edges that cut through everything you touched like that air does, where would you go? Right! You'd head straight for the Rio Grande Valley. There's always a warm sun, luscious fruit trees, and a lazy lifestyle down in the valley."

"And so it goes. Ever since the very beginning of time, the air we've got here has rushed all over the state. Freezing, raining, fogging, rustling, whistling, roaring, teasing, testing, and tormenting, but always staying right here. To my knowledge, the only air that has ever left Texas was inhaled by a traveler as he crossed the border and exhaled on the other side."

UFO
IN
SOUTH
TEXAS

A BOUT AN HOUR OUT OF HOUSTON, I HAD JUST
passed the Junction VOR. The Beechcraft Baron, showing
240 knots on the DME, was streaking for El Paso. Flying
alone in the early morning had always been a delight to me, but
this was one of those special mornings that linger in the memory.
The strong southeast winds that hurried me along carried volumes
of moisture that only yesterday had been part of a great swell in
the Gulf of Mexico.

The rising yellow and orange fireball behind me lit the sparkling
blue sky and reflected off a brilliant white stratus layer below. There
was an unrippled smoothness to the ride, and the undercast had
the same smooth flatness in all directions. Although the Baron was
eating huge chunks of south Texas, it was easy to imagine being
suspended motionless in space above a frozen white planet.

Years of training warned me that the lack of apparent motion
and the comfort of a smooth ride eroded the sky search for other
airplanes. Redoubling my efforts, my eyes roamed from wingtip
to wingtip. The visibility was limited only by the capability of my

eyes. Scanning the endless blue and white around me, it seemed that I was the only thing moving in the whole universe. I had not seen another airplane since liftoff. Then, suddenly, there it was.

It was just a black speck against the smooth flatness of the stratus tops. The speck appeared slightly below the stratus horizon and many miles away. Gripping the glare shield, I pulled myself forward, trying to get a few feet closer. I squeezed my eyelids down, trying to bring the pencil point ahead into better focus, but the speck remained a speck. It had no apparent size or shape.

With the autopilot doing a good job of splitting the airway and holding my 8,500 feet, there was little else to do but relax and speculate on what the speck might be. At first, I didn't consider that it might be anything but another airplane. Because it was only slightly below me, I reasoned that this speck was an IFR flight at 8,000 feet. Traveling the same airway in the same direction meant that our closure rate would be slow, or perhaps would not occur.

Although I was annoyed at not being able to distinguish any shape for the thing, I tried to forget my unknown companion by establishing another position fix. Because I was on the airway, the DME told the whole story, but I wanted to waste as much time as possible, so I tried triangulation. Tuning the San Angelo VOR north of my course, I centered the needle and found that the DME position agreed with the triangulation within a half mile. I scanned the engine instruments. All the gauges were in the green as the Baron blistered the miles.

Looking ahead once again, I was surprised to see that the unknown object was no longer a speck; I was closing in on it. Although it was still specklike, it displayed a definite roundness; it certainly didn't have wings. It was difficult for me to accept the roundness because I had already convinced myself that it was an airplane. Slowly, I accepted the fact that it was not an airplane. I strained my eyes for better resolution, then rationalized that it must be a helicopter.

Because of our altitude difference, it was certain that my unidentified companion would disappear below the Baron's nose before I could make positive identification. The circumstances seemed to justify a slight (500-foot) infraction of the VFR cruising rules. Starting a descent to 8,000 feet, I knew that I could get a little closer by exchanging altitude for a momentary increase in speed. The DME indicated 260 knots as I leveled the airplane at 8,000 feet directly behind the increasing size of the thing that I now visualized as a helicopter.

As planned, I gained some distance during my descent. The object now appeared about the size of a dime viewed from across a small room. From this distance I should have been able to make out the rotor disc and perhaps the landing struts of a helicopter; there were none. That perfect roundness persisted. Reluctantly, I conceded that it was not a helicopter. Grasping for an explanation, I momentarily thought of a free balloon. No, it was not a balloon. Most balloons have a pear shape, and I was close enough to have seen the *gondola*, or instrument package, if it was a balloon.

A little confused and without any idea as to what the thing might be, I realized that the closure rate was increasing. As I drew closer, the object took on a silvery metallic appearance and occasionally reflected the morning sun back toward me. It now appeared about the size of a nickel viewed at arm's length and it was getting a little too close.

I was close enough to distinguish objects protruding at right angles to each other out of the round shape. However, I was too close, so I turned the Baron slightly to the right and planned to pass close enough to get a good look. The oblique view from my new position off the airway, and to the side of the thing, was startling.

The ship wasn't round at all. It only looked round when viewed from directly behind. The true shape was ellipsoidal, much like a long football with blunt ends. It had four enormous fins jutting out of its rear, some with flashing lights. There was a cabinlike structure on its underside containing a row of windows. Emblazoned on its silvery side in huge graphics was the enormous word GOODYEAR.

Knowing that a rare encounter like this should not be passed too quickly, I eased back on the throttles. As the Baron's speed fell below gear speed, I cranked out the rollers. The speed continued to fall as our closure rate decreased. When the speed was below flap speed, I dropped full flaps and nursed the Baron down to minimum controllable airspeed. With everything hung out and as slow as I cared to go, I still zipped by this lethargic giant of the skies.

I could see two faces shining out the cabin windows with hands waving a gleeful hello. Knowing the courage that it must take to face hundreds of miles each day in a 30-knot machine, I returned the aviator's traditional sign of respect, the hand salute. Cleaning up the Baron, I continued toward El Paso, pleased that such a special close encounter had happened to me.

MURPHY'S LAW

S PURRED BY THE PROSPECT OF BEING ABLE TO FLY, I had worked long hours in helping Bo repair the damage to his homemade biplane. To this point, the work had progressed smoothly. All that remained was to straighten and re-cover the vertical fin and rudder. Using my father's hand-powered forge, we heated the bent areas, and slowly, carefully straightened them. We were ready for covering.

Mrs. Cravens, who by this time had developed quite a fondness for Bo, was cheerfully on hand to help with the fabric covering. I wondered if she really enjoyed the airplane work, or if she just wanted to be around Bo. Whatever her reasons, the three of us made a good team. By the time the covering of the vertical fin neared completion, we had learned what each of us could do best. I commented, "You know, we're getting real good at this dope and fabric work. We should finish this without a hitch."

With his head still bowed toward the work, Bo looked from under his thick eyebrows and said, "I wouldn't count on not having any hitches, boy. You've always got to allow for Murphy's Law. And don't you *ever* forget it!"

"What's Murphy's Law?" I questioned.

Giving me one of his "I'm-surprised-you-didn't-know-that" looks, Bo replied, "You mean you don't know Murphy's Law?"

"No sir," I innocently replied.

"It's simple, boy, but always true. Murphy's Law says that if anything can go wrong, it will."

Mrs. Cravens rested briefly from stitching the fabric and said, "I have never heard it called by that name, Bo, but it always works like that for me."

There was a pause in our conversation for several minutes as we stretched and stitched the fabric over the remaining portion of the vertical fin. At the end of her row of stitching, Mrs. Cravens dropped her hands into her lap and asked, "I wonder where a thing like that comes from?"

After a pause, Bo answered, "Well, ma'am, I suppose having things go wrong has been with us ever since the first man. Just look what happened to Adam and Eve. We didn't get around to putting a name on it until much later."

Bo took a deep breath that swelled his chest, exhaled slowly, and said with a sigh, "I can't be sure about this, you understand, but I'd bet your bottom dollar that it was named for B.L. Murphy."

"Who is B.L. Murphy?" Mrs. Cravens asked.

"You mean *was*, ma'am. He's gone now."

Bo gave the impression that he didn't want to go any further, so I probed, "Well, who *was* he, then?"

Breathing deeply again, Bo continued, "I first met B.L. in the fall of 1916 when we was training for the war. At that time he looked like he had already been through two and a half wars. He claimed to be 29 years old, but looked like he was 69. His hair was all gray and he spoke with a stutter. He was an awful, busted up, crooked mess."

"Now Bo, you aren't going to tell us another of your tales, are you?" Mrs. Cravens grinned.

"Why ma'am, this is serious business. This boy has got to learn about such things if he's going to fly airplanes."

Eager to hear Bo's story, I encouraged Bo. "Tell us some more about this B.L. Murphy, Bo."

"Well, his trouble started the very day he was born; it was his name. He told everybody that his ma named him Benjamin Lee after her favorite history people: Benjamin Franklin and Robert E. Lee. But those of us that knew B.L. real good always believed that his initials stood for Bad Luck."

Mrs. Cravens and I chuckled at each other, but I was quickly scolded by Bo. "Don't you laugh, boy; this is serious business.

Before B.L. was out of his diapers, the Murphy house burnt to the ground. It was the coldest night on record, in February of 1887. The temperature was hovering below zero and the wind was howling. Old man Murphy wanted to leave the fireplace lit all night, but Mrs. Murphy was against it.

"'A hot coal may pop out onto the floor and set the house on fire,' she had said.

"But the old man closed up the front of the fireplace with a screen and said, 'There, that'll fix it. Nothing can go wrong now,' and they all went upstairs to bed."

Bo fell silent as he helped us fit the fabric around the difficult curve of the rudder. We were hanging on the edge of his story not knowing how the Murphy place caught fire. I couldn't stand the silence and was about to ask what happened, when Bo said, "The screen worked real good. Not a single hot coal popped out on the floor. But, on that last stoking of the fire before going to bed, old man Murphy had knocked a brick loose at the back of the fireplace. The hot air and flames leaked out the back and played directly on the wooden framework of the house. When the Murphys awoke, the whole house was aflame and their bedroom was filled with smoke.

"B.L. was the only one to get out alive. The old man was the first to go; he was trying to beat a path through the flames for Mrs. Murphy and little B.L., but was overcome by the smoke and fell down the burning stairway. Mrs. Murphy made it back to the bedroom with B.L. in her arms, but by now, they were completely surrounded by flames. She wrapped B.L. tightly in two or three blankets and charged through the flames. She crashed through the bedroom window as her nightgown and hair burned. They bounced and rolled to the roof's edge and fell 10 feet to the ground. She fell right on the baby and was dead on the spot. Her body smothered out the fire, but B.L.'s little arm and shoulder were crushed. It never did heal right and from that day on it was real crooked and a lot shorter than the other."

While Bo stopped to breathe several deep breaths, Mrs. Cravens said, "Bo, that's a terribly sad story. Did that really happen?"

"Sad indeed, ma'am, but there's more to it yet. B.L.'s life was just one calamity after another.

"Being without parents, he had to be raised in an orphanage. That wasn't no fun in those days. The boys would sometimes fight over the food because there wasn't enough to go around. Oh, they wouldn't fight in front of the ladies, or in the dining room. They had all their fights settled amongst themselves before mealtime. That's how B.L. lost half of his ear. He and another boy was rolling around in the dirt clawing and clubbing at each other. B.L. got in a couple of lucky kicks and was getting the best of it when the other boy chomped down on his ear. The boy didn't bite his ear off, but it was mangled up so bad the doctor had to cut some off to save the rest from infection.''

As if a twinge of pain shot through my ear, I instinctively reached up to reassure myself of its well-being. My release of the rudder fabric to feel my ear was timely. The stitching was complete and it was time for the first coats of protective nitrate dope. I opened the can and asked Bo, ''What happened then?''

''When B.L. was about your age, boy, the orphanage let him out to a farmer that needed a good hand. The farmer had agreed to provide for B.L., as long as he was a good, hard worker. That farmer was an ornery old cuss, but his mule was even worse. B.L. didn't get along with the mule any better than with the old man. It seemed like the farmer wanted B.L. to work like a mule, so, when he worked hard enough to satisfy the farmer, the mule resented it and looked for a way to kick B.L. smack into the middle of next week.''

''I know the type,'' I joined in. ''We've got this one ornery old cow. Everytime I milk her she tries her best to bite me or kick me. I can get a bucket of milk out of her, but I always come away bleeding or bruised.''

''Well then, you know how B.L. felt. He was working just as hard as the mule because he didn't want to have to go back to the orphanage.

''Now, the mule didn't like it one bit, but he didn't show it. That mule was a cagey old fox. For several days the mule acted friendly and cooperative. He did everything that B.L. wanted, and he did it in the nicest and politest way that a mule can. Just when B.L. began to relax and trust the mule, it happened.

''When the mule saw that B.L. wasn't looking, he turned about half sideways and let loose one of those double-footed, lightning-bolt kicks. If he had caught B.L. square, his head would still be rolling down the road somewhere. As it turned out, B.L. took a glancing blow across the bridge of his nose. The whole front of his face was smashed.

"That darned old man he worked for was either too mean, or too tight, to take B.L. to a doctor. He got the bleeding stopped by taping down the whole front of B.L.'s face. For a while, he looked like a mummy. The only problem was that the shattered nose got squeezed off to the right side of B.L.'s face, and that's how it healed. Ever since that day, B.L. would look one way and sniff another."

Mrs. Cravens sat up straight from the dope work and said with unusual firmness, "Now, Bo, don't you go telling things like that if they aren't true."

"Well, ma'am, I wouldn't think of such. I know all this to be true because B.L. told me himself. What I can't explain is how he lost three fingers off his right hand; all he had left was his little finger and a thumb. He never would talk about his fingers, but I heard some talk about how his leg got bowed out, and what made his foot point the wrong way. Some folks say that as the years passed, B.L. was getting serious with that farmer's young daughter.

"She didn't seem to mind his terrible looks, but the farmer was downright irate about it. He considered B.L. far too ugly and unlucky for his daughter. They say after the farmer refused to let them see each other, there was talk of an elopement. They say there was a big fight and after the old man got B.L. down, he ran over him with his heavy plow horse. They say he broke B.L.'s legs in three or four places. But I've always considered that just so much gossip and don't care to pass it along."

"That poor man," Mrs. Cravens sympathized.

"Well, you're right about that, ma'am. That poor man just drifted from one disaster to another. Everything he did would sooner or later turn sour, then he joined the air service. In the service, he found one thing that he could do better than anybody else."

Mrs. Cravens interrupted Bo by saying, "I'm certainly glad that he found something he could do. Was he a pilot like you, Bo?"

"No ma'am. He was too chopped up, busted up, and put back crooked for that. He was the list keeper!"

"List keeper? What's a list keeper?" I asked.

"Well, boy, in those days we didn't know very much about building airplanes. Everybody was experimenting with different kinds of wood and metal and fabric, and the way of making things and hooking them all together. We had trouble with everything from the landing gear to the propeller, from the engine to the control wires, from the instruments to the tail wheels—I mean everything! If it didn't break, it would quit working or stop running. So they gave B.L. the job of keeping a list of everything that went wrong with our airplanes.

"The idea was to change the way of making something if it kept causing trouble, or to keep it the same if it worked well. There was nobody as good as B.L. at this job because he had a real knack for finding things that went wrong. He poked and prodded all over the airplanes after each flight. He would grill each pilot and mechanic; and he could even find foul-ups that had been unnoticed by others. He was so good at this, he soon had a list of foul-ups that would fill a thick book. It was about this time that the captain decided to send him, and his list, back to headquarters. And that was the last ever heard of B.L. Murphy."

"You mean he ran away?" asked a wide-eyed Mrs. Cravens.

"Oh, no ma'am, he wouldn't do that. They were going to fly him to headquarters and he was anxious to go. You see, he had some plans of his own. I can remember talking to B.L. just before the takeoff. B.L. and I was close—well, as close as you can be to somebody like that. He would say things to me that he wouldn't to others. B.L. said to me, 'I kn-know you pilots dr-drew straws to see who had to fly me back, B-Bo.'

"And I said to B.L., 'Ah, it ain't like you think, B.L.'

"B.L. said, 'I-It's OK, B-Bo. I kn-know you pilots think m-m-my initials stand for B-Bad Luck. Wh-wh-when I get to h-headquarters, I'm going to have my n-n-name changed to Ga-Ga-Gordon.'

"I says to him, 'Ah, B.L., you don't need to do that. Changing your initials to G.L. won't change a thing. You'll be all right if you just give yourself a chance.'

"I could see that my words didn't do any good on him. Anyway, off they went and sure enough, something went wrong along the way. Nobody knows for sure why, but the airplane crashed. Both B.L. and the pilot died, but they never did find B.L.'s list of things that go wrong with airplanes."

"Do you think it blew away in the wind?" I asked Bo.

"No, boy. It was much too big and heavy for that. Some say that B.L. Murphy's spirit reached down from the clouds and scooped it up. Some say that he's still flying around up there with that list under his arm. Some say that just when a pilot feels fat and sassy and thinks nothing can go wrong—just then, B.L. Murphy's spirit, with that long list of trouble, settles into the cockpit. Boy, when that happens, if there is anything that can possibly go wrong, it darn sure will."

THUNDERSTORM
IN THE
CACTUS

WHEN IN EL PASO, I ALWAYS GO TO THE OLD CAC-
tus Saloon. With its thick adobe walls and narrow,
board-covered windows, it resembles an old fort. It was
built sometime before the Civil War when it was a hangout for hard-
drinking badmen. On many occasions, it was the scene of violent
knife- and gun-duels between rival outlaw bands, both Texan and
Mexican. It is one of the places where the legend of courage and
marksmanship held by the Texas Rangers was born and grew. More
than once a lone Texas Ranger faced a group of outlaws in a raging
gun battle.

Back then, it was almost a day's ride on horseback out of El
Paso along the Rio Grande; today it's across the street from the
airport: now it's called the Cactus Bar.

Although the city has reached out to engulf the Cactus, the
bar retains its one-hundred-proof early Texas atmosphere. It is
dimly lit by the small amount of late afternoon sunlight that can
slant through its small windows, and unairconditioned and musty.
You can sit within its dark recesses and imagine the life-or-death
struggles that took place there.

Its ancient woodwork carries reminders of its past.
"RUSTY-1882" is carved in the tabletop where I place my cup of
coffee. Through the dim and heavy atmosphere, you can make out
holes from bullets that frequently hailed within its walls.

The Texas Rangers and badmen are gone now. The Cactus is

often overlooked by the casual tourist, but it is always crowded with a mix of pilots from the airport and cowboys from nearby ranches. The cowboys come not to fight, but to play in the loud and rough manner of their ancestors. The clash of knives and the roar of pistols have given way to loud and boastful bragging.

As I sipped my coffee during one visit, lost in the nostalgia of the surroundings, a tall and lanky figure rambled into the Cactus, pushed through the noisy crowd, and took a chair at my table. He wore heavily scuffed boots that reached almost to his knees and overlapped his tattered blue jeans. His faded plaid shirt and strong odor attested to his long hours and hard work under the sun. His cheerful red face was topped by uncombed, carrot-colored hair. Pushed jauntily to the back of his head was a sweat-stained, broad-brimmed cowboy hat. He oozed the sights and smells of a real working cowhand.

"Howdy," he said while taking his seat at my table.

"Howdy," seemed to be a fitting reply.

Ordering a large mug of beer, he added, "They call me Red."

"Pleased to meet you, Red. I'm Sam."

"I see by your hat that you're from the airport."

Recalling that I was wearing a baseball cap that said 'Beechcraft' across its front, I answered, "Uh-huh."

"You a pilot?" he probed.

Not wanting to give too much away until I knew what was about to take place, I mumbled another, "Uh-huh."

"Well, I ain't no *real* pilot, but I can fly a airplane."

"Oh?" I inquired with interest.

"Yeah, I started taking lessons while I was working on a ranch out west of Austin, but I never could pass that durn written. Took it seven times! I just give up and quit trying."

Drinking in about half of the beer in his mug and wiping his mouth on his shirtsleeve, he continued, "Whew! Dust and heat, heat and dust. Texas sure can dry a man out. Yeah, I quit taking them lessons, but kept on flying. I flew a old Cezzner One-Forty that we had on the ranch. It didn't have no annual or nothing, but that didn't bother me none because I didn't have no medical or license. I'd filter our tractor gas through a shimmy cloth to full it up, and then fly that rascal. Man, me and that little old airplane was a pair!"

I mumbled another "Uh-huh," and sipped some coffee while he gulped the rest of his beer.

Wiping his mouth on his shirtsleeve again, he shouted, "Hey, barkeep, bring me another one of them beers." Turning his attention back to me, Red continued, "You know, when you live near Austin, you can get all heated up about the University and the Longhorns. Well, the Longhorns was going to play the Rice Owls down in Houston that year. Both of them was real good and they was playing for the championship. I just had to see that game. You see, I'm a real football nut."

He sucked down another half mug of beer and continued, "Well, you know from Austin to Houston in a old pickup is a pretty good haul, so I decided that I'd go in that little Cezzner. By the time I got one of the Mexican talked into going with me, we was running late. The kickoff was at two P.M., and I knew we wouldn't have no time to eat, so we bought some sandwiches, milk, and orange juice. I threw it all on the hat shelf behind the seat and helped the hand buckle in.

"The weather forecast was for F and D, you know, fine and dandy—and when we took off from Austin, it weren't too bad. It was about 2,000 foot scattered with a thin overcast layer at about 8,000 foot. The wind was calm from the north and the visibility was great; you could see as far as you could look.

"I climbed the 140 up and got between them layers at about 3,500 foot and headed down the highway for Houston. Things was going great until we got to Smithville, and there that lower layer started closing up. Well, I ain't no fool, so I got down under them clouds where I could still see the highway.

"I was going along at about 1,500 foot, having a good time telling the Mexican all about how the 'Horns was going to stomp the Owls, when I noticed them clouds just getting lower and lower. And the bad thing about it was that the visibility was dropping because it had started to rain. Well, the next thing I knew we was just about in the treetops trying to stay below them clouds. And what's worse, I couldn't see a thing because it was raining hard by now, and I knew the pressure was dropping too. In fact, the pressure got so low, it was sucking up dirt and leaves right off the ground."

I blinked my eyes while making an effort to unscramble what Red had just said about the pressure, but was interrupted.

"Well, we was about twenty miles the other side of Smithville and things was getting worse. It appeared to me like them clouds went all the way to the ground just ahead. I sure didn't want to hit a tall tree or something else down there, so I decided to climb back up and get between them layers again. Oh, I knew I wouldn't be able to see the highway from up there, but that's better than hitting a tree or something."

I had to agree with that and nodded. Red drank some more beer and continued. "We was climbing through the soup and I felt a lot better when the altitude meter started showing a thousand foot again. Now you might be wondering how I was able to climb up through them clouds without a horizontal guide-ro."

Leaning close to me as if he were about to reveal a closely guarded secret, he said, "Well, I'll tell you a thing I learnt from a old cropduster: When you get in them clouds, you just watch the compass. It'll tell you which way you're going like always, and it'll too tell you when you ain't level! You just watch that little round part with the numbers on it that tells the north or south and if it tilts—you're banked and have to straighten up."

I couldn't believe what I had heard. Red was attitude flying on a liquid compass! He was also revved up now and there was no stopping him. Swigging his beer and wiping his mouth again, he continued. "Well, when I got back to 3,500 foot, there weren't no opening between them layers, and the rain was really pouring down. I figured that lower layer had just got a little thicker, so I decided to keep on climbing. If I couldn't find that opening, I'd just climb up on top."

"On top?" I thought. Knowing how suddenly a towering thunderstorm can develop in that part of Texas, I would have bet that the tops easily reached 30,000 feet. But Red was excited and continued.

"Well, when I got to 4,000 foot, it got real dark. I mean it was *black* in there! And it was raining so hard that it just made a roar, I couldn't even see the prop. Then, KAPOW! We almost did it right there on the seats! A lightning bolt went off like a cannon; I mean it exploded! It was like turning on a million searchlights inside of that cloud. And then it began to lightning here and there, all around us. Bam! Pow! Pow! Man, I've been to two side shows and a circus and ain't never seen nothing like that. Just before one of them babies would pop, it turned everything blue, and the hair would stand up all over my body. When a real big one would pop, I'd get a look at the Wet. Everybody know most Mexicans are sort of dark brown in color. This one was kind of greenish white! But I figured it was that funny blue light that made him look that way and kept on climbing."

Using a great deal of hand and body motion that rocked the table and threatened to spill my coffee, Red added, "The airplane was bucking like a wild horse because it was getting pretty rough in there. At about 5,000 foot, up through the blackness, I saw a real bright spot in the cloud. It was the sun shining down through a hole in the cloud, which meant we were getting close to the top. I headed for the bright spot, planning to break out on top, but I never got there. At about 6,000 foot a air pocket grabbed us and threw us into a toronated turn."

My ears and eyebrows must have perked at the same time because in all my years of flying, I had never heard of a "toronated" turn. I would have asked about it, but Red bubbled over again. "Well, after that turn, my compass was spinning like the wheels on a outlaw slot machine. I didn't know which way was which, and I lost sight of the bright spot. Since my passenger had never flown before and looked a little nervous, I told him that I was doing a good job of flying and that he should relax.

"I no sooner got them words out of my mouth when we was hit by one of the worst terminals you'll ever hear about, no matter how long you fly. We was climbing at about 4,000 foot a minute and the airplane was rolling around so much I had a hard time reading the gauges. By steadying my eyeballs across the end of my nose, I could make out the airspeed; it was 180. Since that's over the red line by a good bit, I thought it would be a good idea to pull the power back. When I got the engine down to idle, the airspeed dropped to 120, but we was still climbing at about 3,000 foot a minute, so I decided to push on the wheel to get the nose down."

At this point I was wondering if Red knew down from up, or any other direction, then he answered my question. "Well, that must have been the wrong thing to do because we lost all of our gravity. The sandwiches, milk, and orange juice started floating around the cabin. The sandwiches didn't bother me none, but in those days they put milk and orange juice in real glass bottles. If them two happened to get together, we'd be in trouble."

"In trouble?" I thought. This guy was already up to his eyeballs in trouble and didn't know it.

Slugging down more beer and speaking at a faster rate, Red continued. "I let go of that wheel real fast because pushing it over caused so much trouble. I started grabbing for the milk and told the Mexican to see if he couldn't catch some of them sandwiches. Meanwhile, we was still being knocked around and still going up.

"When the altitude meter went past 11,000 foot, I heard the awfullest rattling and pounding ever. It was hail! The rattling was just little hail about the size of a pea and nothing to worry about. The pounding was hail about the size of a orange that weren't froze hard. It was like being hit with big snowballs.''

Having survived a damaging hail encounter myself, I listened with keen interest. ''I was afraid that if we went any higher them big ones would freeze hard and cause us trouble. It was cold up there. It was so cold my hands was plum blue and I thought the blood in my feet was going to clogulate. Ice was building up all over the wings and ice started freezing up my tarpeetic tube, and when that happens you lose all your airspeed. And when you lose all your airspeed, the old airplane ain't flying no more. I've been in some bad IRF conditions before, but this was the worst. I gave the compass my 100 percent divided attention and knew I had to do something to pull us out of that mess. I twisted on the wheel, but nothing happened. My elerons weren't froze up; they just quit working for some reason. Things was really bad now, but I didn't let on so as to scare my passenger. But I knew durn good and well that I was going to have to put it into a spin and spin out the bottom of the storm.''

I almost choked on a swallow of coffee as his words hit me. ''Spin out the bottom?'' He just said the clouds went all the way to the ground.

With a grim look to match the tenseness of his words, Red sipped some beer and went on. ''I jerked the wheel back all the way hard, and stomped the left rudder full. I just locked the controls like that and waited. Well, I knew that something was happening because the milk tried floating around again, but I couldn't tell which way we was turning because my compass was spinning to beat sixty.

''I saw by the altitude meter that we was still going up and we passed 15,000 foot. I was real worried now because at them high altitudes you can get high noxeeum real easy, and that takes all your senses away so you do some dumb things. I knew that if we was up there very long, we'd have to open the windows to let in some more oxygen so I could think of the *smart* things to do.''

My mind swirled with what Red had told me thus far, but based on the fact that he was here to tell the story, I knew he had somehow survived. I was anxious to see what smart thing he had done to get home safely. Red supplied the answer.

''I just held the wheel all the way back and full left rudder and, sure enough, the airspeed fell and the altitude started coming down. I got the Mexican to sit on them sandwiches and hold the milk and orange juice in his lap. He was real happy to have something to do. I just held on and let her spin down through the hail, lightning, and rain. I was planning to let the altitude meter unwind to about 2,000 foot, let go of all the controls, and put the power back on so she would fly herself back to straight and level. But when I got to 2,000 feet, the engine was dead—I forgot to put on the carburetor heat and it was froze up solid. I weren't worried none, though, because I had just practiced emergency landings the week before."

Spinning at 2,000 feet with a dead engine through a thunderstorm that reaches the ground is hardly a normal mode of flight. I thought to myself, "This guy doesn't practice emergencies, he creates them." I braced myself for the conclusion of the story.

"I just held it locked in the spin and, sure enough, I came out the bottom of the clouds with about 300 foot to spare over the trees, but the engine was still dead. I started looking for a place to set it down, and would you believe the luck? There was a little airport just under my left wing. Why man, that was a piece of cake. I just wheeled it over and dropped it right on that runway.

"It turned out to be the Smithville airport, which I had already passed 10 or 15 minutes earlier. I still ain't figured out how I traveled 20 miles backwards. Anyway, in about 15 minutes the ice melted from the carburetor and the tarpeetic tube. I got her going again after a few tries, but that Mexican said he didn't want to go to Houston, and he didn't want to go to Austin. He said he'd stay right there in Smithville. Well, I told him that except for a little mustard on the headliner, there weren't a thing wrong with that airplane, but he still wouldn't go. Well, as you can see, the whole day was ruined so I just come on back to Austin by myself."

I didn't know if Red's story were true or not, but one thing was certain: Red had somehow learned about the inside of a thunderstorm. If it were just loud talk, no harm had been done. If it were true, however, I needed to be careful. In Red's eyes, I was a *real* pilot. I didn't want to say anything that might encourage him to make another flight into instrument conditions, especially into a thunderstorm.

While Red waited for my reaction, I summoned all the strength of those brave lawmen who made the Cactus Bar safe for me and Red. I turned to him with the straight-faced, steely-eyed calm of a Texas Ranger facing a battery of outlaw guns and said, "Who won the football game?"

FIRST FLIGHT

WE WERE BETWEEN THE MORNING AND AFTER-
noon milkings. The Saturday sun was high, the sky was
clear, and the wind rolled gently from the southeast. It
was a perfect day for flying. Grumbling something about it all being
nonsense, father had agreed to let Bo and me take time away from
our dairy chores for my first airplane ride.

While father continued his work at the dairy, mother
accompanied Bo and me to the pasture in which the freshly repaired
biplane had been parked and tied. As the three of us approached
the biplane, I felt a terrible uneasiness. My apprehension was not
about the airplane ride; I had waited eagerly for this moment and
looked forward to the excitement. Bo had told me that he was going
to let me handle the controls, and I was worried that my performance might disappoint him.

Bo and I slowly circled the biplane for the preflight inspection.
Step by step, he explained how to inspect its controls, its structure,
and its engine. We checked the fuel quantity and sampled the fuel

for any sign of contamination. At the conclusion of the preflight inspection, Bo turned and faced me. He placed his hand on my shoulder, looked squarely into my eyes, and said, "Boy, don't you ever leave anything to luck or take anything for granted in an airplane. You check it!"

"Yes sir," I quivered.

"Now get up on that wing and I'll help you into the front cockpit."

I climbed up on the lower wing. Mother reached out, squeezed my hand, and said, "Sam, you pay attention to Mr. Wages and do whatever he says."

"Yes ma'am," I answered while trying to prevent a quiver in my voice from exposing my nervousness.

I had climbed into the front cockpit many times while we were rebuilding the damaged biplane. I had sat there with stick and throttle in hand dreaming fanciful dreams of soaring through wind and cloud, of banking and turning, of rolling and diving through wide blue skies. But now, faced with the reality of actually having to manipulate the controls in flight, I trembled and fumbled with the seat belt.

"Here, boy, let me help you," Bo said, pulling the seat belt tightly around my hips. He pulled an old cloth flying helmet down around my ears and said, "Buckle it under your chin." While I was buckling the helmet's chin strap, Bo sent a thrill through me by strapping a pair of real aviator's goggles across my eyes.

Bo mounted the rear cockpit, giving me time to study my surroundings. Sitting in the front cockpit was like sitting in a large wooden barrel with eyes just above the rim. The view ahead was completely blocked by the huge radiator that was necessary to cool the Ford V-8. The radiator extended from the fuselage to the upper wing, so I would have to learn to live without forward visibility. The upper and lower wings prevented me from seeing up or down, so by stretching upward and to the left or right, I could get an angling view of a small area ahead and to the left, or right, of the airplane.

Inside the cockpit, there was very little to study. Directly in front of me was a large wooden instrument panel and, except for the three words "SOLO REAR ONLY," the panel was completely bare. A thick, baseball-bat type of stick jutted between my legs. There was a large pair of rudder pedals that I could just reach with my toes. The throttle lever was beside my left thigh.

"You ready, boy?" came from the rear cockpit. I nodded.
"Well, take hold of the stick and throttle and get your feet on the rudder pedals."

As I took the controls, I felt the stick move fore and aft. Bo said, "When you feel the stick move like that, it means that I will fly the airplane and you just relax and follow me on the controls. Understand?" I nodded and felt the stick move left and right. "When you feel the stick move left and right, it means you will fly the airplane and I will relax on the controls. Understand?" I nodded again.

As the moment of flight drew closer, a lump developed in my throat. "This isn't going to be just an airplane ride," I thought. "He's going to ask me to fly this thing." The biplane suddenly looked very big and very burly.

Bo shouted, "Clear," as a warning to any bystanders that he was about to start the engine. He engaged the starter and the propeller began to turn. I followed his motions as the throttle was pumped from full closed to full open, again and again. The engine made one or two muffled belching sounds, and black smoke rolled out of its exhaust pipes. Then, with a tremendous roar that surprised me, the Ford V-8 came to life shooting short orange flames from its exhausts.

Running unsteadily at first on five or six cylinders, the V-8 shook the whole airplane. Wind and oil-laden smoke swirled through the cockpit, while the strong vibrations engulfed my body. Then, as all eight cylinders came into full play, the engine smoothed out, and the twin exhaust stacks played parallel symphonies of explosion and flame.

Without brakes, the biplane began to bump across the pasture toward the take-off point. Bo zigzagged the airplane in order to see what was ahead. He looked left while weaving right, then looked right while weaving left. I duplicated his body motions, leaning left and right as the airplane weaved through graceful arcs.

At the north end of the pasture, we turned into the wind. I could see mother standing in the distance off to our right side. She seemed to be a great distance away, and I was tempted to raise my hand to wave. This temptation quickly ended when my left hand was carried forward with the throttle; the engine roared to full power. A chill trickled down my spine, and my right hand unconsciously gripped the stick tightly.

The biplane rolled forward, gaining speed. The stick glided smoothly to its full forward position, the tail of the biplane lifted off the ground, and the airplane assumed a level attitude. Racing forward on the main wheels with the tail high in the air, we quickly passed my mother's position. From the corner of my eye, I could see her waving.

The engine roared. The wind whistled. The wings developed lift and the wheels danced lightly through the grass. Then, WHUMP, a small bump in the uneven pasture bounced the airplane into the air. The stick moved smoothly back to a more neutral position. The wheels settled back into the grass with another WHUMP and once again bounced into the air. The stick came back a little more and we were free of the earth. The pasture faded away below.

At first there was only the pasture, but as we climbed my view expanded to neighboring farms. I followed the motions of the stick and rudder pedals as Bo smoothed several bumps in the air. Higher now, I could see for many miles. My head and eyes spun from side to side absorbing the expanding view below. We continued to climb and I realized that the temperature was falling as a chill swept over me.

High in this cool blue sky, it seemed that I could see from the Red River on my right to the Rio Grande on my left. It seemed that we were miles high, and I imagined that the whole state of Texas was in clear focus below me. Later, I learned that we had climbed only 4,000 feet and that the visibility was no more than 50 miles.

The nose lowered to the horizon and the Ford eased back to a more relaxed purr. We flew level for several minutes as I continued in my amazement at being able to see so much so clearly. For my 13 years on the surface, the earth had seemed crowded, cluttered, confining, and in some places even dirty. Peering down from the freedom of the sky, though, it was different.

The whole world seemed divided into neat rectangles, sliced squarely by crisscrossing roads, and dotted by distant towns. It all seemed so clean, so structured and meaningful. The air was cleansed and freshened by its 4,000-foot separation from the earth. I deeply inhaled the cool sweetness of altitude. The graceful arcing turns made by Bo and these enthralling sensations hypnotized me. I seemed to lose touch with reality. Then a startling thought came to me. "Any minute now, he's going to wag the stick sideways, and I'm going to have to fly this thing."

Bo made a series of gentle turns. The left turns were always followed by right turns. Then the nose moved smoothly up and smoothly down. It seemed that Bo was saying to me, "This is how it's done," as I followed his control motions. My mind turned from the engrossing sights around me to a study of the control motions and resulting airplane motions. I had no sooner begun to concentrate on flying when it happened. The stick vigorously wagged from side to side and then went limp. Every muscle in my body tensed, my eyes went to a squint, and my stomach gripped as I assumed command of the biplane.

At first, I thought the best thing was to hold the controls firmly in place and simply fly straight ahead. But as the seconds slowly ticked away, the right wing started to descend and a gentle right turn developed. Around and around we went. I was embarrassed by this unplanned turn and decided that I should do something to correct it. Cautiously and rigidly I pushed the stick to the left. The biplane began to recover from the unwanted right turn, but to my surprise, the nose came up and we started to climb.

Engrossed with this unexpected development, I neglected the changing bank and fought to return the nose to level flight. As the nose came back to the desired position on the horizon, the bank continued to change and a left turn developed. I stiffly jerked the stick back to the right. The biplane rolled out of the left turn and into a right turn as the nose zoomed up again. I continued to fight the stick right and left and up and down as we wallowed our way through the skies.

Bo allowed me to fight the controls and wobble along for about fifteen minutes. (It seemed like fifteen hours of hard work.) But, slowly, I began to get the feel of the biplane and was learning just how much control to use. Our flight path became steadier and I began to feel a little smug. However, when the stick jerked fore and aft, I was more than ready for Bo to again resume control of the biplane.

I relaxed and a wave of exhaustion flooded my body. Each muscle had been tensely knotted against its opposite. My heart was pounding and I gulped in air as if I had run the same distance we had flown. Now there was nothing to do but relax and enjoy the scenery during the return flight to our pasture landing strip. Or so I thought!

Suddenly, the Ford roared up to full power and Bo lowered the biplane's nose well below the horizon; we were in a power dive. Until now, the flying wires between the wings had produced a reassuring hum; now, they began to scream as altitude and power were converted into speed. As our speed built to a terrifying point, the wires screamed louder and louder. I had the feeling that a great disaster was about to occur. I imagined that we were going 400 or 500 miles per hour, and that we would soon smash into the earth. My body tensed for the imagined impact, but the stick glided smoothly back and the biplane soared into an enormous loop.

As we arced upward, the G forces pulled my body. At the top of the loop, the G forces almost disappeared. I raised my head and saw the inverted earth directly overhead. Most of our speed and power had been converted into altitude, and we seemed to hang motionless, G-less, for a brief moment at the top of the loop. Bo eased the engine back to idle power and the biplane smoothly arched earthward. Our altitude was converted back into screaming speed.

Recovering to level flight imposed heavy G forces. I felt my cheeks tug downward and had difficulty keeping my hands on the controls. I tingled with excitement.

I couldn't believe what I had just been through and thought " . . . sure wish we could do another loop." Then, as if in response to my silent wish, the engine powered up to a roar and the nose went down again. "We're going to do it again!" I happily thought and the same sequence of events followed. The speed built to the point where the wires were screaming loudly. The stick came smoothly back. The G forces tugged at every part of my body, and the biplane arced upward. As I was expecting the biplane to smoothly arc over to an inverted position at the top of the loop, the stick eased forward. We broke out of the loop into vertical flight. We were going straight up!

Perpendicular to the earth, the biplane and its little Ford engine clawed for altitude, but try as it might, the biplane could not overcome the earth's pull. Gravity gradually won the tug-of-war. The sound of the wires told me that our flying speed was rapidly diminishing. The G forces were easing. An electrifying shock ran through my body as the stick wagged left and right. I was again being told to fly the biplane—but how?

The nose was pointed straight upward, the engine was at full power, and the airspeed had all but disappeared. I was confused and hesitated as the biplane staggered to zero airspeed and began to fall backwards through its own exhaust. The engine bucked, sputtered, surged, and occasionally spit large balls of smoky orange flame as the carburetor refused to work in this unusual attitude.

There were no G's and then there were negative G's. It felt as if my eyeballs were going to float out of my mouth and then as if my stomach was going to squeeze my brains out through my ears. Through a bewildering confusion of sensations and emotions, a compelling thought came to me. "Bo's expecting me to do something!" Then, an instant later, "Get the nose down! Push the stick forward and get the nose down," I thought and thrust the stick forward.

Falling vertically backwards had reversed the function of the elevator. I was surprised when the biplane wallowed over onto its back. Instead of having the earth under my feet as planned, it was once again overhead. I heard laughter coming from the rear cockpit. As we fell earthward upside down, I recognized that my situation looked just like the last half of the loop that Bo had done earlier. I quickly duplicated the control motions that he had used during the loop.

Pulling the throttle back to idle power position seemed to soothe the bucking, stammering engine. Pulling smoothly back on the stick caused the biplane's nose to arc earthward. The speed and G forces built and I continued to pull back on the stick. Holding the wings as level as I could, the biplane soon returned to normal flight conditions. The stick jerked fore and aft, so I released control to Bo.

Totally exhausted now, I was happy to see that Bo was headed back to our pasture for a landing. I relaxed in the hope of regaining enough strength to learn something about the landing from his control motions. As we approached the landing field, I stretched my tallest and leaned left in an effort to see the field a little better. The wires hummed low-pitched pleasing sounds as the earth rose to greet us. The biplane floated inches above the grass as the stick glided smoothly back, and power was reduced. Then, WHUMP, with one small bounce we had landed.

From that day forward, without hesitation, I knew that I was to fly airplanes. It was the thing for me to do.

MY
SPECIAL
TAILGUNNER

GIVEN A CREW, AN AIRPLANE, AND TIME IN WHICH to train, the thoughts and actions of ten men can be blended into that remarkable unit called a *combat aircrew*. This kind of closeness and interdependence takes effort and develops slowly. It begins in the early training days when the newly formed crew is brought together and told, "Gentlemen, this is the B-17 Flying Fortress. You are going to fly it."

I had always visualized it happening that way, but I was wrong. The luxury of blending a well-trained crew with a fresh airplane only became possible late in the war after the supply of men and equipment exceeded the demand. During the late months of 1942, the U.S. Army was struggling to get its bases established in England. The runways were built first so we could start our bombing missions. We lived in tents and there was a serious shortage of trained men. The Army grabbed anybody willing to man a station, stuck him in whatever would fly, and sent him up against the Luftwaffe and the flak.

MISSION NO. 13

Although I have never been superstitious, this was my thirteenth mission and I felt uneasy about it. My crew was composed mostly of untrained and untried volunteers. The airplane had been severely damaged on earlier missions and was quite a question mark itself.

As we climbed through 8,000 feet over the English Channel, I glanced at my copilot, Bill Jackson. I had met him only the day before and had no knowledge of his flying skills. Anxious to see what he could do, I allowed him to make the take-off. His technique was uncertain, with several pitch oscillations that bordered on being dangerous; I thought this was because he was fresh out of training and on his first mission.

Most of the other crew members were strangers to me and had little or no combat experience. The notable exception was Charlie Johnson, the top gunner and engineer. Having already completed 22 missions, Charlie was the most experienced combat crewman on the base. On several missions, he and his pilots had nursed badly damaged airplanes back to England. With injured crewmen and engines out or smoking, the crews brought their birds home on knowledge, skill, and determination. Charlie knew everything there was to know about the Flying Fortress and all of its systems. I felt comfortable having him onboard to help me keep a wounded B-17 in the air, if need be.

The opposite side of the coin, however, was my tailgunner, Kubiac Poppenski. Because of his graying hair, we called him "Pop," but no one really knew him. He wasn't even in the Air Corps. Pop had been an artilleryman in the Polish Army. When the Germans overran Poland in 1939, he lost his wife, his children, and his home in one bitter blow. He had been defeated in combat and driven from his homeland. Embittered and determined to fight the Germans, he fought in western Europe with the English troops in 1940. There, too, he was defeated. He was part of the army driven against the sea at Dunkirk. Miraculously saved from the German onslaught by the famed Dunkirk Evacuation, he had waited in England.

Because the land war against the Germans in Western Europe was still some time away, there was no use for a Polish artilleryman who could speak only a little broken English. But I have never seen a man with such an intense hatred for the Germans. He wanted to destroy as much of Germany as he could and kill as many Germans as possible.

With that level of desire, he had little trouble getting himself assigned to the U.S. Army. In 1943, all the U.S. Army had going was our B-17 strikes. So there he was, not knowing the first thing about airplanes, sitting in the back of my B-17 guarding our fanny.

The rest of the crew varied in skill and experience between my "proven" top gunner and my "Lord-only-knows" tailgunner. Anxious to get a feel for the crew, I said, "You stay with it, Bill. I'm going to have a look around."

Knowing that our initial cruising altitude was to be 18,000 feet, I picked up a portable oxygen bottle as I slid out of my seat. Working my way through all the tight spots in the B-17's nose section, I chatted with each crewman in the forward compartment. Squeezing past the 8,000 pounds of explosives in the bomb bay, I noted many nasty-looking repairs that had been hastily made. This Fortress had had her tail feathers scorched and showed the scars of violent combat. Wondering if all the patches were going to hold together, I slipped into the aft crew compartment.

I was going to talk with the waist gunners and the ball-turret operator, but I didn't intend to crawl back to the tailgunner's station to see Poppenski. It was just too tight to squeeze back there, and Poppenski couldn't speak enough English to get much past "Hello".

During my conversation with the gunners, one of them interrupted our chatter with a wave of his hand. He pressed his headset closer to his ears for a moment and then said, "Sir, they want you up front. Lieutenant Jackson says they have some kind of trouble."

"Let me have your headset," I said, taking the man's headset and mike. "Whatta ya got, Bill?"

"I don't know exactly. There's something wrong with this airplane. We're having a heck of a time keeping up with the formation," came Bill Jackson's worried reply over the intercom.

"What does Charlie say about it?"

"He says everything's in the green and looking good, but we're having to pull extra power. And something else, Skipper . . . I've used up all the nose-down trim just to keep her level."

"You guys hang on up there. I'm coming up," I said, thrusting the headset and mike back at the gunner. My inexperienced gunners had concerned looks on their young faces. Trying to make my words sound like a reassuring command, I said, "Don't worry about the airplane. I'll take care of it. We'll be in their fighter range soon. You guys keep those fighters off our backs. Don't get wild and waste your shots. Be steady. Plan your lead angles, wait until they're in range, and then let 'em have it."

Back up front, I found that Charlie was right. All four Wright Cyclone engines were grinding away just as advertised. The temperatures and pressures were normal. In fact, you couldn't ask for four sweeter sounding or smoother running engines. However, they were running at 80 percent power.

"Bring 'em back to our planned cruise power," I said. A subtle change in the engine and propeller noise I had become so accustomed to told me that Bill had responded.

"Let me take it, Bill," I said to my copilot while sliding into my seat.

"If we pull 'em back to cruise power, we can't stay up with the formation, Skipper," Bill said with a worried look.

"If we don't pull 'em back, we won't have enough gas to get home. Now what's this about the trim?"

"Well, look at it. It takes all of the nose-down trim." Bill replied.

With the engines stabilized at our planned cruise power setting, I began to spin the trim wheel fore and aft.

"No doubt about it, Bill. This thing does take a lot of nose-down trim," I agreed and then added, "Feels like an aft center of gravity. See how light the control forces are and how wildly she responds."

"I thought it might be something like that because my take-off was hard to control, but it just can't be, sir. Herb did the loading."

Herbert Tollison was our bombardier. I knew that he had supervised the loading, but remembering that he too was just out of school and that this was his first mission, I pushed the intercom button and said, "Herb, did you see anything funny about our load? It seems that we have an aft c.g. problem."

"No sir. It's a uniform load. They're all the same kind of bombs. We could put them anywhere in the bay and we would still have the same condition." Herb answered.

"Well, there's something wrong."

As we continued to discuss and analyze our problem, we were falling farther and farther behind the formation. I was reminded of this fact by two sources. Bill was saying, "If we fall much farther behind, we'll be a sitting duck out here by ourselves," when the squadron commander broke in on the radio to say, "You're out of formation, Hawkins. Pull it in tight."

"Yes sir," I replied, then told Bill, "Don't worry. Let's go to climb power until we catch up and then try about 80 percent again. As soon as we get stabilized in formation, let's get a handle on our fuel burn and see how far we can go like this."

A tight formation of B-17s can direct an enormous amount of firepower at an enemy, and we needed to be in a tight formation because we began to sight the first group of enemy fighters.

"Sir, I know what it is!" Bill chirped.

Looking quickly and directly into his eyes, I didn't need to ask, "What?"

"It's this airplane. The Krauts have blown this crate out of the sky twice already, and those monkeys back at the base have patched it back together crooked. There's no way for this thing to fly right."

"Maybe," I conceded.

"I think we should drop this load and return to base." Bill pleaded over the hammering of the fifty-calibers as the fighters swarmed over us.

"Too late, Bill. If we turn back now, those fighters will chew us up. We need the formation now." Trying to ease his fright with humor, I added, "Besides, if we don't drop this load on some Kraut, that pole in the back might cut our throats."

Without fighter protection, our only defenses were the fifty-caliber machine guns and our tight formation. The Messershmitts disregarded these defenses and swirled all around us. They came in waves of six to eight planes with guns blazing, and then regrouped while others were attacking. There was no letup and they played no favorites. Each plane in our formation was repeatedly sprayed with machine-gun and cannon fire.

Showers of enemy bullets easily ripped through the thin aluminum skins of every Fortress in the formation. I could feel the pain and death around me as we grimly pressed toward the well-guarded target. First one Fortress, and then another, and another, burst into flames and spiraled earthward. Although we saw some parachutes, whole crews were lost in some bombers.

We were going to northeast France to destroy a foundry that was casting engine blocks for German tanks. The fighters were determined to stop us. They dealt their miseries all the way from the English Channel to within about ten miles of the target.

As we neared the target, the fighters turned us over to the boys with the 88s, and they were enjoying their work. With a powerful cannon like the 88, they could sit on the ground in complete safety and shoot as hard and as fast as they liked. There was nothing we could do. In order to provide a good bombing platform, we were on autopilot and had to fly straight and level as steadily as possible. We could take no evasive action. There was nothing to do but continue toward the target.

We had lost several planes to the fighters, now the 88s which were radioed our altitude, airspeed, and heading by enemy aircraft trailing us—were taking a terrible toll. The ugly black puffs of exploding cannon shells surrounded and engulfed us. Each crew in the formation was pressing their ship a little harder, hoping to somehow outrun the fury surrounding them. Throttles were unconsciously pushed forward.

Our ship was heavily raked by fighter fire, and now shrapnel from the exploding 88s whistled and ricocheted through the cabin. One blast shattered the left aileron and the Fortress wallowed toward the left. Another blast demolished the autopilot gyro near Charlie Johnson's feet. We would have to hand-fly our Fortress the few remaining miles to the target. The flak thickened, and blast after blast ripped our ship. She was crippled and staggering.

"We've got to have a little more power," I pressed.

"They're on 90 percent now," Bill gulped.

"Well, let's see what they'll take," I said while pressing the throttles full open. We were pressing a battered airplane to the limit, asking her to somehow hold together and whisk us away from danger. I was thinking, "If we can just get out of the drop zone with enough power left to stay in the air, we might have enough gas to get home," when a strange thing began to happen. The closer we got to the target, the more balanced the airplane became. The control forces gradually returned to normal, and the ship's response improved and became positive. I found myself repeatedly reaching for the trim wheel to take out some of the nose-down trim fed in earlier.

Then we were at the drop point and in an excited, high-pitched voice, Herb said, "Bombs away!" Suddenly free of its heavy burden, the Fortress gave a lurch and seemed to be catapulted upward and forward. The altitude jumped and the airspeed began to build. I was twirling the trim wheel again and said, "Bay doors closed."

Bill threw the switch and we heard THRUMP, THRUMP as the doors closed. As the 88s continued to pound on us, the formation rolled left to depart the drop zone to the northwest. A preplanned descent of 2,000 feet to throw off the 88s began, and I said, "Let's get the power back. This thing's about to run away with us." I was surprised by my own words because just a few minutes ago we couldn't get enough power and trim was nearly impossible.

While we were busy over the target, the fighter jocks had refueled and rearmed, and were waiting for us. As soon as we were out of the range of the 88s, the fighters pounced on us again. Despite the considerable damage our airplane had suffered, the engines had escaped untouched. Our ship was performing so well we could have left the formation behind. However, the fighters always came down hard on the bombers that had lost engines and fell behind. Our strength remained in a tight formation, so we slowed with the rest of the group to help protect the tail-enders.

The airflow past the hundreds of holes in our ship made a whistling sound easily heard over the roar of engines and clamor of machine guns, but we had plenty of power, we were trimmed properly, and we were flying well. From all the excited chatter on the intercom, punctuated by an occasional Polish curse word, I could tell that my entire crew had somehow survived the beating. All gunnery stations were exchanging vicious blows with the Messerschmitts.

As the fight boiled across France, the fuel gauges showed near empty. My rapidly disappearing fuel worried me more than the fighter bullets tearing at our plane. Then abruptly the fighting stopped. Having exhausted their fuel or ammunition, the fighters disengaged and turned away. The crew fell quiet and relaxed. After a long moment of silence, Bill leaned close to me and said, "Whew! Am I glad it's over."

"It ain't over yet, Bill. We're almost out of gas. Let's squeeze 'em down to economy cruise. Hey, Charlie, you know this bird better than anybody else, so give me a guess on how far we can get like this."

As the Wrights smoothed back to a relaxed purr, Charlie read the gauges, twirled his computer, and penciled on some paper. Finally, he pressed the intercom button and said, "We can't make it back to the base, sir. Just no way. We can't make enough speed for the gas we're burning. We're going to be short by fifty miles or more."

That meant we would go down in France—territory completely held by the Germans.

"Ok, Charlie. She's flying good. I'll lean these babies back the best I can and fly a straight line to England. You go back and plug up the holes in the skin to reduce the drag. Stick seat cushions in the big ones and cut cloth patches from shirttails to plug the smaller ones. That'll get our speed up. With a little luck, we might be able to stretch it to the French coast."

Charlie rushed away to start plugging the holes, while I pondered the difference between going down in the middle of France or on the coast. I had just decided that it didn't matter since we would be taken prisoner either way when Tubbs, my right waist gunner, chirped on the intercom, "Any of you guys ever think about swimming the English Channel?" I was grateful for Tubbs and his cheerful attitude. The whole crew picked up his spirit and began joking back and forth as they worked on plugging the holes.

I strained for maximum fuel economy. Western France suddenly seemed as big as west Texas as mile after dreadful mile slowly slid beneath us. Soon we sighted the English Channel many miles in the distance. The fuel gauges were bouncing unsteadily on empty. I radioed my condition, announced my intention to try for an auxiliary field along the English coast, and asked for the Air-Sea Rescue to stand by in case we went into the water. Reluctant to give up precious altitude, I started a gradual letdown.

It seemed an eternity to the French coast, but we had made it to the water's edge. The channel stretched before us. As we ventured out over the water, with fuel gauges now firmly on empty, we counted individual waves that seemed to move faster than our plane. Each man reviewed both bailout and ditching procedures. I switched on the intercom and said, "You guys stand by to bail out. If these babies quit, don't wait for my order, just jump."

We could see the English coastline miles ahead. Each man in our wounded bird looked longingly at it and wished mightily for the safety of its smooth beaches. Our eyes switched nervously from the coastline ahead to our now dead fuel gauges. I had all engines throttled well back, trading altitude for distance while saving fuel for the landing. Then finally Bill spotted the auxiliary field in the distance.

"There it is!" He shouted and pointed.

It was Waterloo Auxiliary Number Three. It wasn't much. It was just a long, flat spot along the English coast. There were no buildings, no vehicles, and no people, but it was the best looking thing we had seen all day. I ordered the crew into crash-landing position and prepared for the worst. On our long final approach, the number three engine coughed and sputtered into silence. Pulling the propeller into feather, I said to the crew, "Too low for a bailout. You guys hang on. We'll make it."

I gripped the wheel, trying to squeeze a little more life into the running engines. Two miles from touchdown, number one began to miss and sputter. As I feathered the second engine, Bill said, "Come on, baby, just one more mile." Bringing the power up on the two remaining engines would burn more fuel, but I needed the extra power for altitude and speed control. The landing gear rumbled into down-and-locked position. Striking the water now would tear the airplane apart. Survival would be nearly impossible.

With the rest of the crew tucked tightly in crash-landing position, Bill and I were the only ones at our stations. Our teeth were clamped tightly, our muscles tensed hard, and our eyes squeezed to slits. We were prepared to hit the water, rather than the beach. It was going to be close. Then by some miracle the wheels rolled onto the loose gravel surface. The remaining engines sputtered, surged once, and spun silently to rest. The entire crew seemed to sigh. The relaxation was so great that I could feel it ripple through the steel and aluminum. The Fortress coasted slowly to a stop. No brakes were needed. I leaned back with closed eyes and exhaled deeply. The tenseness ebbed.

Bill wakened me with, "What the heck happened out there today, Skipper? Going in we had a dog that wouldn't fly right, and coming out she was all beat up, but ran like a racehorse. We could have outflown anything in the formation. What happened?"

"I don't know, Bill. Let's talk about it tomorrow."

MISSION NO. 14

The Germans had ridiculed the concept of daylight bombing and said that they would make our bombing raids too costly to continue. For a long time it looked like they were going to do it. The cost of the last mission was seven known dead, seventeen injured, and six planes lost. Of the sixty men to go down with those planes, only eleven parachutes were counted. All sixty would be listed as Missing In Action since no one was willing to admit the worst.

Of the twenty-two Fortresses that made it back, nine would be out of commission for several weeks while repairs were made. Our airplane was among that group. The maintenance crews had refueled our Fortress at the auxiliary airfield and flew it back to the base. Once again they began patching her up. We paced restlessly up and down the flight line because there weren't enough flyable B-17s to go around.

During this lull we had an opportunity to inspect our airplane thoroughly. Bill inspected it, Charlie inspected it, and I inspected it. We had hoped to find an explanation for its peculiar flight characteristics on the last mission. We all found the same thing: nothing! Other than looking rather rag-tag because of the many repairs (she now had patches on some of her patches), everything looked like it was supposed to look and worked like it was supposed to work. Our test flight proved the same thing; she flew beautifully. Our only problem was that we had no autopilot. A piece of shrapnel had smashed the autopilot gyro and there were no replacement parts.

Since we had done so well on the previous mission (meaning we made it back), the group commander reassigned us as a unit to the next mission, saying, "I know you don't have an autopilot, Hawkins, but we need that airplane. You just hand-fly it in formation and drop your bombs when we do."

The crew liked flying together again. They felt that our Polish tailgunner brought us good luck. Pop had become a beloved part of the crew and the crew was becoming a team.

We were together again in the same airplane, but the target was quite different this time. Some guy in Air Command dreamed up a screwy plan to interrupt the food supply to the German foot soldier by bombing canning factories. With a bellyful of 250-pounders, we were on our way to bomb what we called "the sauerkraut factory" somewhere in southern Germany.

It was an exciting occasion for most crews because this was the first official raid on German soil, and the longest to date. We would fly nearly eight hours. During the mission briefing, they told us that the Germans would not expect this kind of attack and that there would be very little or no fighter or antiaircraft fire. This was supposed to be a milk run. As we lined up on the runway centerline for take-off, I hoped they were right.

Before the wheels were in the wells, I knew we had trouble. The trim tab control wheel had to be rolled well forward of its normal take-off position, and pitch control was erratic and sloppy. Bill and I looked quizzically at each other. We knew the 6,000 pounds of explosives we were hauling in the bomb bay had been loaded correctly. Along with Herb, I had performed the calculations and supervised the loading of the bombs. I had also directed fuel loading into each fuel tank and ammunition loading at each gunnery station. It was impossible for the airplane to be out of balance. But it was!

"I still think it's this airplane, Skipper. It's just crooked," Bill said in very positive tones.

"No way, Bill. She flew too good yesterday on our test hop. It didn't fly like it was crooked then, did it?" I argued.

"Well, no, but there's got to be something wrong with this airplane that we've overlooked." Bill answered and then fell silently into deep thought.

With all of the nose-down trim applied and no autopilot, forward pressure on the control yoke was still required to maintain level flight. It was a little worse than on the last mission. Also, following the pattern of the last mission, higher power settings were required to keep pace with the formation. My arms were getting tired when the squadron commander's voice came over the headset.

"You O.K., Hawkins?"

Pressing the mike button to answer, I said, "UHHHHhhhh," while I considered revealing the difficulties, but then continued, "Yes sir, we're doing fine."

"Well, keep it in tight just in case we pick up some of their fighters."

"Roger," I answered and then thought, "Sure wish we had loaded a little extra fuel. I'd rather be over gross than out of gas."

We were almost halfway to the target. My arms were aching now and I was about to ask Bill to take it when he suddenly sat up straight and shouted, "I've got it, Skipper. I know what's wrong with this airplane!"

Without giving me a chance to ask "What?" he continued excitedly.

"This airplane has a broken back! That'll explain everything. When we load her down with bombs and fuel, she bends in the middle and flies like a dog, and then," he gulped in a breath of air and continued, "when we burn off the fuel and drop the bombs, she straightens up and flies right."

He was searching my face for a reaction while I considered what seemed to be impossible. However, if it were true, it would explain some of our handling problems. More importantly, it meant that she could break in half at any moment. I made my decision and pressed the intercom button.

"Charlie, come up here a minute." I didn't want to discuss this on the intercom, with the rest of the crew listening.

"Yes, sir," Charlie said as he squeezed between the pilot and copilot seats.

"Bill, you take it while I talk to Charlie. Watch that forward pressure now," I warned, and released control of the airplane.

Turning to place my mouth close to Charlie's ear, I said, "Charlie, Lieutenant Jackson thinks we may have some broken longerons. He thinks she's bending in the middle under load. What do you think?"

The very thought of it jerked him back. His eyes opened a little wider than usual and he said, "Good Lord, I hope not."

"Me too, but it would explain some of our problems. Are there some inspection plates that we can remove to examine the longerons?" I asked.

"Yes, sir, there are a lot of them in the bomb bay."

"If she's busted, that's probably where it'll be. Get some tools and a couple of flashlights and let's go have a look."

As Charlie backed out of the pilot's compartment, I had the feeling that some parts to this puzzle were missing. I was unfastening my seatbelt to follow Charlie when Bill leaned over and said, "Why don't we just drop this load and go home and let the maintenance boys inspect it?"

"Look, Bill, we don't know if anything is busted or not. What we do know is that we flew a good mission in this airplane three weeks ago and she got us home. We've been flying over two hours today and nothing has happened. If we're going to drop our eggs, we may as well do it on the target. Now we're only about an hour and a half from the target and our luck is holding on the fighters. You just keep it in formation while Charlie and I go inspect the longerons. Let me hear from you if there's any change."

I slapped him on the back and winked some encouragement as I backed out of the pilot's compartment to follow Charlie.

We were dismantling our Fortress from the inside. Charlie and I removed every inspection plate and access cover that we could find. Peering through one opening after another, our inspection was inconclusive. Charlie asked, "You want me to start putting some of this stuff back on?"

"No. If this baby is broken, we've got to find it and abort the mission before we get to the target. Just let all that stuff lay for now. See that radio stack over there?"

"Yes sir."

"We could get a lot better look if we removed it. Let's get it out."

The radio boxes were removed and stacked on the bomb bay doors. We could see a good deal more of the lower longerons, but could not find any sign of a crack or break. Dissatisfied, I asked, "Whatta you say we take out these unused bomb racks?" "Whatever you say, sir."

We continued removing every bit and piece of our ship's interior that could give us the least glimpse of the longerons. Then without warning, Bill's voice came over the intercom.

"Ten minutes to I.P."

Charlie and I looked at each other, a little surprised that time passed so quickly, and I said, "I've gotta get back up front, Charlie. You've got about ten minutes before we open the bay doors. Throw all of these loose parts into the aft crew compartment."

As Charlie said, "Yes sir," we heard an all too familiar BOMP followed by BOMP BOMP.

"Flak!" I yelled. "Forget this stuff and let's get to our stations."

As I slid into my seat, I said to Bill, "I bet the Krauts even put 88s around their johns."

"Yeah, but look at 'em. There can't be more than three or four of them down there," Bill said with unusual bravado.

"It only takes one," I thought to myself.

"What did you find in the bomb bay, Skipper?" Bill asked. "Nothing."

The word had just passed my lips when it happened. One of the missing pieces to our puzzle reappeared. The airplane began to fly better. I was reaching for the trim wheel and said, "Look at it, Bill. We haven't dropped our bombs yet and I'm having to retrim. I remember now. This happened on the last mission too. By the time we got to the drop point, we were perfectly trimmed and it's doing it again."

"And our speed's building, Skipper. Just look at it," Bill squealed. Now deeply engrossed in the difficult task of hand-flying a bomber in an effort to accurately place bombs on a target, I retrimmed and mechanically called, "Bay doors open."

Just as Bill hit the switch, I remembered all of the loose parts and equipment in the bomb bay, but FUWUMP PLAP, the doors were open and we sprayed B-17 parts all over Germany. A few minutes later we were over the sauerkraut factory, or whatever it was, and I saw the other planes dropping their bombs.

"Come on, Herb. Let 'em go," I mumbled to myself.

Then, "Bombs away!" Herb answered.

With the weight of the bombs gone and the bay doors closed, our Fortress was performing like a racehorse. Again, we could have easily outrun everything in the formation. However, the possibility of a fighter encounter existed, so we continued in tight formation.

"Let's pull the power back so we don't run off and leave the rest of these guys," I bragged.

The four-hour trip back to England was uneventful. Charlie, Bill, and I spent the time discussing that peculiar experience just prior to drop when our Fort had changed from a dog to a racehorse. As we turned onto the final approach, no one had an explanation, but Charlie did ask me, "Lieutenant, what should I tell the maintenance men when they find all that stuff missing from the bay?"

MISSION NO. 15

"Hawkins," the squadron commander said with his cigar gripped tightly in his jaw teeth, "What are you trying to do? Help the Germans win this war? You left here with a darn good airplane, flew a milk run, and brought back the only damaged ship. The bomb bay was gutted. That airplane will be out of service for weeks. What happened out there?"

I always felt ridiculous standing rigidly at attention in his office while he nervously chewed his cigar and paced the floor, but I tried to make the best of it.

"Well, sir," I began, and slowly, carefully described my experiences on the last two missions. I gave particular emphasis to the fact that the airplane's flying characteristics improved from near-impossible to near-perfect during a short interval just prior to drop. I explained the broken longeron theory and told of our frantic search through the bomb bay. I was hoping that he could explain what was happening.

Instead, he roared, "What do you take me for, an idiot? I have been flying B-17s a long time, and I have never heard anything as ridiculous as that. Now let me tell you something, Lieutenant Hawkins. If you get out there and properly calculate mission fuel and armament, and then supervise the loading of bombs, fuel, and ammo, there is no way for that airplane to be out of balance like you say."

Before I could explain that I had supervised the loadings on the last mission, he raged, "And another thing, Hawkins. There can't be anything cracked or broken in that airplane because we have the best maintenance personnel in the Army. If there was anything broken, they would find it and fix it."

"Yes, sir," I answered, seeing that neither argument nor reason was possible.

"I'll tell you another thing, Hawkins. You and your crew are going to get out there and work right beside the maintenance crew until that airplane is all fixed up." Thrusting his face to within an inch of mine and raising his voice even louder, he added, "And you're going to do it by Friday afternoon. We have a very important target to hit Saturday, and I want to see you right up there in the front of the formation. You tell your men that all passes and leaves are canceled.

"And as for you, I want to remind you that I got you promoted to First Lieutenant just last month. If that airplane isn't ready to go Saturday, you're going back to Second Lieutenant and maybe even back to copilot. Now you get out there and put that airplane back together."

"Yes, sir." I said, saluting and spinning around to leave the room.

"Hold it, Hawkins!"

I froze with my back to him as he continued, "Just to prove my point, I will personally supervise your calculations and loadings on Saturday morning. Now go get to work on that airplane."

We spent the next three days at hard labor and in deep frustration. We had more than enough men to do the work, but couldn't find the parts. New replacement parts for the perfectly good ones that we had dropped in Germany were not to be found in England. Only three ways existed to get the needed parts: order them from the factory back in the states and wait; make new parts by hand; or, steal them from other B-17s. One way or another, we were determined to get our Fortress ready.

The simpler inspection plates and access covers were laboriously fabricated by hand from sheets of aluminum. A few of the more complicated pieces were borrowed from other B-17s that couldn't make Saturday's mission. Bits and pieces of equipment were "liberated" from other aircraft as the opportunities presented themselves.

As the deadline approached, we had about two-thirds of the job completed. As expected, on late Friday afternoon, we spotted the squadron commander speeding toward us in his jeep. The job was far from complete, but we had replaced those parts most visible to a casual inspection. One real concern was the radio stack that we had been unable to come up with. Flying without it would not be dangerous. The missing radio box would only deny us the use of a few communication frequencies. To solve this problem, we built a fake box to look like the radio equipment and braced for the inspection.

"Close the bay doors. He may take our word for it." I said to the maintenance chief. The sergeant, seated at the pilot's station, threw the switch and the doors slammed shut on our secret.

The major wheeled in beside the nose of our Fortress and jumped out before the jeep came to a full stop. Chewing briskly on his cigar, he marched straight toward me. The entire crew came to attention, and I saluted as he said, "Is it ready to go, Lieutenant Hawkins?"

He walked right past me and stopped beside the bomb bay doors.

"Yes, sir," I exaggerated.

"Open the doors and let me have a look," commanded the major.

The maintenance chief looked down at me from the pilot's window as if to say, "Do we really have to?"

I gave a big shrug behind the major's back and said, "Open the doors, sergeant."

The doors opened and the major stepped in to have a closer look. Viewing the aft portion of the bay with hands on hips, he chewed his cigar and said with a half grunt, "HUHMPP."

He then faced forward in the bay, repeated his chewing, and grunted another "HUHMPP."

Walking quickly back to his jeep, he said without looking, "Hawkins, we load at two A.M. Be here!"

"Yes, sir," I said and saluted his departure. The entire crew danced and howled a Polish stomp. We had made the deadline for tomorrow's mission. I was amazed by the eagerness of my crew to face almost certain injury and possible death. We were truly becoming a close-knit combat crew.

We loaded the airplane under the supervision of the squadron commander. The crew briefings were held at four, and we were lined up for take-off at five. The major shuffled our take-off and formation assignments so that I would have to take off immediately in front of him and then fly his wing. It was clear that he intended to keep his eye on us.

My turn came for take-off and I brought the power up full. The Fortress groaned under its heavy load and started slowly. She strained to move forward, first at a creep, then a walk, and finally a run, but with all four Wright engines roaring at full power she should have accelerated much faster. She felt very overloaded and I knew that our problem was with us again, despite the major's supervision. Knowing what to expect, I rolled the trim tab control to its full nose-down position. As the speed slowly built up, I eased forward on the control yoke expecting the tail to come up, but nothing happened.

Farther down the runway at an even greater speed, I tried again with the same result. The tail would not come up. The Fortress raced toward the end of the runway as the airspeed neared flying speed; we had used far too much runway. There was panic in Bill Jackson's face as he gripped his seat's armrests and tried to pull the airplane into the air. The main landing gear was trying to lift off the runway, while the tail wheel continued to hug the ground.

As she danced and skidded lightly sideways on the mains, I forcefully jammed the yoke full forward. The tail sluggishly lifted. We ran into the grass off the end of the runway as I studied the obstacles ahead. We were 56,000 pounds of men, metal, and explosives hurtling along at 120 miles per hour. There was no room to stop; she had to fly. Gently coming back on the control yoke, I muttered, "Come on, baby...fly!"

The tail wheel slammed back into the grass as the mains came off. She porpoised through several wild pitch and yaw oscillations. The situation was deadly serious, and control was nearly impossible. I fought the controls trying to stabilize the airplane and keep it in the air. We gyrated over the fence at the edge of the base and headed directly toward a group of buildings.

"Get the gear up!" I shouted at my wide-eyed copilot.

As I fought to steady our flight path over the rooftops, the gruff voice of the squadron commander barked over the radio, "What kind of take-off was that, Hawkins?" Struggling to prevent a disaster, I didn't answer. I had all that I could do just flying the airplane. She was worse than ever before. She was definitely unstable and trying to do cartwheels in the sky. We battled her instability throughout the climb as the formation began to take shape.

We managed to form up with the other B-17s and climb to 22,000 feet. Flying level now, we were in the front rank of the formation off the left wing of the squadron commander. Things had settled down and were manageable, but we were having to pull about 85 percent power just to stay even.

So much forward pressure was required on the control yoke that both Bill and I were holding it. Things were so bad that the autopilot could not have held it if we had one. I was getting a little mad over not being able to determine what was wrong with my airplane and said, "Bill, can you hold it? I'm going to have a look around."

"I don't know if I can hold it for very long. This thing is getting worse on every mission. Why don't we drop this load while we're still over the Channel and go back home?"

"That's no good, Bill. If we drop the load, she will start flying right again and we may never know what the problem is. You just hang in there and I'll get Charlie to help you."

Pressing the intercom button, I said, "Charlie, come up here for a minute."

As Charlie came forward, I said, "Charlie, get in my seat and help Lieutenant Jackson fly this thing. Just follow his lead and you'll do fine."

I was determined to diagnose the problem. The loading had to be correct; it was calculated and supervised by the squadron commander, the copilot, the bombardier, the crew chief, and myself, so I eliminated that from my thinking. I was also convinced that the airplane was not crooked and that nothing was broken. The trouble had to be something else, and I was determined to find it.

I began my inspection in the nose of the airplane at the bombardier's station and planned to search every inch back to the tail gun. Working my way slowly through the airplane, I examined each crew station and each crew member. The bombardier, the navigator, and the top gunner checked out, as did their stations and equipment.

I completed the forward section and found nothing. The crew was right. Their equipment was right. The airplane was right. Getting even angrier, I plunged into the bomb bay, believing I would find the trouble there, but we had inspected and reinspected every rivet while on the ground and they all checked out again in the air. Finding nothing in the bomb bay and feeling frustrated, I entered the aft crew compartment. I examined the radio operator and his equipment. I studied each gunner and each gunnery station. Nothing. Everything checked out perfectly just as it did on the ground. That left only Poppenski.

By this time I was tired. Despite the subfreezing temperatures at our altitude, I was perspiring freely and my frustration had dissolved into disgust. Breathing through the small portable oxygen bottle only made matters worse. I was in a terrible mood and didn't feel like squirming through the small tunnel back to the tailgunner's station. With a forty-five strapped on one hip and an oxygen bottle strapped on the other hip, that crawl would be nearly impossible. Besides, we had checked the tail section several times on the ground and it was ok, too. Stewing in my disgust, I was turning to make my way forward when I recalled something my old flight instructor, Bo Wages, told me years earlier: "Don't ever leave anything to luck or take anything for granted in an airplane."

I turned and began my tight crawl through the tunnel back toward Poppenski. The only obstacle in the tunnel between the tailgunner and the rest of a B-17 is the big hump that houses the tail wheel when it retracts. Once past this hump, the going gets easier, but my passage was nearly blocked by a second obstruction. Trying to squeeze by this second obstacle in the near darkness of the tunnel, I discovered by feel, more than sight, that this second hump was a huge pile of rocks.

"Rocks!" My mind recoiled in disbelief.

It couldn't be. I picked up several of the rocks, which varied in size from a large grapefruit to a small watermelon. It couldn't be. I didn't believe it, but it was. Looking two feet farther up the tunnel, I could see Poppenski grinning at me.

"Poppenski!" I screamed in anger.

"Ya, ya, Capa-teen."

"What are these rocks doing in my airplane?"

Patting his twin fifty-caliber tail guns, he said in Tarzanlike grunts, "Little guns go back. No down. Rocks kill 88s."

"You mean you've been throwing these rocks at the antiaircraft guns as we go over the target?"

"Ya, ya. Guut idee, huh?"

I was staggered. Poppenski had placed us well over maximum gross weight and dangerously aft of the center of gravity limits and he thought it was a good idea.

"No! No! It's a terrible idea. Poppenski, we can't fly like this. We're overweight and out of balance. You dump these rocks overboard and you do it now," I commanded.

I could see that he didn't believe me. We had already flown two missions with the rocks and had proven that we could fly with them. But Poppenski was a dedicated soldier in any man's army, and reluctantly began to comply with my order. With a sorrowful face, he opened his escape hatch and began dropping the rocks. As he slowly dropped one rock after another, I asked, "Poppenski, that's got to be 400 or 500 pounds of rocks. How have you been getting them in the airplane without me knowing it?"

Speaking through his obvious disappointment in me, he said, "Bums lodud—crew go meet. Others coffee. Poppenski put rocks."

It dawned on me that because he knew nothing about our airplane, or our missions, I had allowed him to skip the briefings. About halfway through his pile of rocks, he stopped and looked at me for a reprieve. The hurt in his eyes expressed his pleading better than words. I couldn't stand it and said, "OK, Pop. Pick out two big ones for the 88s—but only two!"

Poppenski broke into a big grin, carefully selected two good-sized rocks, and dumped the rest overboard.

It was a tough mission. We took a terrible pounding and lost some airplanes and crews, but our battered old bus, with Poppenski and his rocks guarding our fanny, took us through it and brought us home safely.

THE
COST
OF
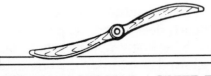
FLYING

BO WAGES HAD AGREED TO GIVE ME FLYING LESSONS in exchange for my help in restoring his homemade biplane. Actually, "give" is the wrong word. Bo made that very clear when he asked me, "How are you planning to pay for these lessons, boy?"

"Pay?" I gulped. "You told me you were going to give me my lessons for helping you fix up the airplane."

"So I did, boy, so I did, but I was talking about my time as your instructor. I'll gladly give you that, but it takes money to keep this airplane in the air."

Searching for an escape from having to pay, I countered, "Well, I think all my work was worth more than just your time."

"And it was, boy. You was a big help and it would have taken a lot longer without you, but you've already been paid for a good bit of your work."

"How do you figure that? I ain't been paid nothing."

"Sure you have. While you was working, I was teaching. Right now you know more about the insides of an airplane than most pilots, and you have a running start at being a darn good airplane mechanic. All that knowledge will stay with you the rest of your life. That's worth a lot right there."

He had me. He held all the aces and I held nothing. He had the only airplane within hundreds of miles, and I was foaming at the mouth to learn to fly. Concedingly, I said, "Well, if I have to pay for the airplane, how much will it cost?"

Accepting my concession with a friendly smile and patting the biplane gently, he answered, "This thing burns about five gallons an hour when everything's working right—there's a dollar right there. And then the oil, it takes about a quart every hour—that's another two bits. And the wear and tear, don't forget that. That's worth another dollar. And no telling what else if you let it get away from you and tear it up. That's worth another dollar an hour. Let's see here, I think that comes to $3.25 an hour."

"$3.25 an hour! I can't pay that much, Bo. I only get two bits a day for my after-school chores."

Bo shrugged and said, "So where's your problem? Two bits a day is $2.75 a week. That'll cover one lesson every other week, with money left over."

"But, Bo. I want to fly every day."

"Every day? Well, that's going to take a lot more money. Do you have any savings?"

"I've got a little, but I was saving to buy Christmas presents for everybody."

"That's mighty nice, boy, and shows that you're growing into a fine man. Things like that make you special, and I won't take your Christmas money. I'll make a special deal just for you. I'll put the gas in before the lesson, and you fill it up after the lesson. We'll let it go at that unless you tear it up. Then you pay for all the repairs. How's that?"

"That sounds o.k. to me, Bo. Let's do it," I said. So my flying wouldn't be free, but I could learn to fly for the cost of the fuel. I thought this meant that he would fill the tank before my lesson and that I would pay for the fuel used during the lesson. It actually turned out a little different.

The fueling/refueling pattern that developed was exactly the reverse of what I thought. Invariably, when it was time for my lesson, the biplane would be near empty. This was a direct result of Bo's popularity. Word that his airplane was once again flying had spread across town and to all the neighboring farms. He was doing a brisk business of sightseeing, cow hunting, and girlfriend buzzing. He was getting $2.00 a ride and burning a lot of gas.

At lesson time, we would fly the nearly empty biplane up the county road, land near the Texaco station, and taxi up to the pump. Bo would jump out of the biplane and say to the attendant, "Howdy, Homer. Put five gallons in it for me, would you?" And he would pay for the five gallons. Following the lesson, we would again land and taxi up to the pump. Bo would remain in his rear cockpit and say, "Fill her up, Homer. This one's on Sam." And I would have to pay for the twelve to fifteen gallons pumped into the tank.

At first, I quietly accepted this routine because students rarely question the mysterious ways and words of their flight instructors. Accepting each motion and utterance as aviation gospel, I quietly and politely paid for all of his business flying fuel while he was paying for my training fuel. It wasn't long before my small savings felt the pressure. I was timidly searching for a way to ask about the refueling routine that wouldn't anger Bo or threaten my flying lessons.

We had just finished my fifth lesson. Homer had taken my money for the thirteen gallons pumped into the biplane. Bo was in a jovial mood because it was a particularly good flying day and I had done well during the lesson. I could always tell when I had done well because he did very little shouting and pounding on the side of the airplane.

"I'm right proud of you, boy. You did real good today. I think you're getting your control coordination down pretty good. Do you have any questions?"

I thought it might be a good time to ask about the refueling and started almost apologetically, "I did have a question, but it wasn't so much about flying as it was something else."

"What is it, boy?"

"Well . . .," I paused for a moment and almost backed out.

"Don't be bashful. Come on, let's hear it," Bo urged.

"Well, it's about the gas. How come you always get five gallons and then, when it's my turn to pay, we get twelve or fifteen gallons?"

Bo's response to my question was instantaneous and very graphic. His face contorted with great shock and then changed to express his surprise that I should ask such a dumb question. Then, as he prepared to answer, his look gradually changed to a gravely serious one. He said, "I would fill it up before the lesson if I could, but I just can't. It's those training maneuvers, boy. Doing tight turns and zoom climbs with all that gas would bust our ballast. You sure don't want to do that, do you?"

Much impressed by the seriousness of his expression and the obvious importance of such a dangerous thing as the ballast, I answered, "No, sir," with firm conviction. I had no idea what the ballast was or the consequences of its bursting, but student pilots often feel compelled to hide their ignorance from their instructors. I did.

"Good! Let's don't have any more talk about this gas business then," Bo said.

I accepted the fact that it would cost me more to learn to fly than I had first thought, and silently determined that I would ask the school librarian to get me a book on airplanes so I could learn about the all-important and dangerous ballast.

Some weeks later, the book arrived on loan from the state library in Austin. It was a marvelous book. It was a large book—eight by eleven inches and about three inches thick. It was bound in a heavy and impressive cloth-covered, hardback binding. The book had been published in 1929 and was an aeronautical glossary entitled *The International Dictionary of Aviation*. Each page was filled with alphabetically arranged aeronautical terms. Each term included a complete description and a small sketch that clarified the description and located the item on, or within, the airplane. I was thrilled when I realized the tremendous amount of aeronautical knowledge that I held in my hands. Quickly leafing through the "B" section, I came to the word *ballast*.

Ballast (bal'- əst) n. Heavy metal bars, usually lead, affixed to the airplane structure to assure correct balance.

"What? There must be some mistake," I thought. "There's no way to bust a lead bar by filling the fuel tank," I reasoned. I scanned the B's again, thinking that I had misunderstood the pronunciation or the spelling, but my eyes always returned to: "Ballast (bal'- əst) n. Heavy metal bars...." There was nothing else that even looked or sounded like *ballast*. The awareness of Bo's trickery slowly emerged in my mind.

My first reaction was one of disbelief. "Surely Bo wouldn't do a thing like that to me," I thought. As the realization of his trick became clearer, my feelings quickly grew into anger. I mumbled, "That dirty son-of-a-gun!" and visualized myself storming up to Bo and denouncing him as friend and instructor.

Fortunately, this response was not immediately possible because school would not be dismissed for several hours. Such a denunciation would doubtless put an end to my flying lessons. I reconsidered my response.

The afternoon classes seemed to drag on endlessly, but as they did, my anger eased. In fact, I came to realize that had Bo not tricked me I would not have seen the aviation dictionary. Although still upset, I was thankful for having discovered this wonderful book.

By the time classes were dismissed for the day, I no longer felt any hostility toward Bo. There just wasn't enough room in my mind for anger and all of the new things I was learning from the dictionary. I was absorbing each and every word in this newly found treasure of aeronautical knowledge. Riding home on the school bus, I decided to say nothing about the ballast, but to continue paying for the extra fuel. After thinking about it, it seemed a small price to pay for my newly gained knowledge, and I was going to fly regardless of the cost.

BUSTER'S BIRD DOG

THE 80,000 ACRES OF THE CALLAHAN RANCH SPREAD in all directions below as the Piper Aztec gently descended through cool fall skies. Old man Callahan once raised vast herds of Longhorn steers on this land. Now its numerous oil and gas wells produce a much greater wealth than cows, and the wells require a lot less work. A small herd of Longhorns has undisputed run of the small pastures around the main ranch house. This to-ken herd is on hand to remind the Callahan heirs of their beginnings.

The remaining ranch lands are used for hunting these days. As chief pilot for the Callahans, I had flown their important and not-so-important guests into the ranch to hunt deer, antelope, cats, javalinas, and all manner of birds. Today's load of lesser lights was half drunk and rowdy. They were going to hunt whitetail dove.

As we banked left entering a base leg to the south runway, one of the hunters identified Shorty's pickup headed toward our landing site. Shorty was a small, shy, quiet man, a good man. He was the type that loud rowdy men liked to bully. As if on cue, the loudest of my passengers, seated directly behind me, leaned forward and shouted in my ear.

"Hey, pilot, whataya' say we give Shorty a buzz job? I mean really blow him off the road."

His whiskey-laden breath floated through the cabin. Taking great pains to fly as smoothly as possible and making a precise base-to-final turn, I let my flying say "no" for me. Old loud mouth sensed my negative response and resorted to bribery.

"Come on, man. I'll give you a hunnerd dollar bill to buzz him good."

I throttled back a little more and hit the gear lever. As the gear clunked into down-and-locked, loud mouth blankly stared at the three greens and realized that his chances of buzzing Shorty were running out. Encouraged by his constantly jabbering buddies, loud mouth now resorted to ridicule.

"You ain't no *real* pilot. They only keep you around because you was with the old man. You're just like them Longhorns: old and useless. You ought to stick to flying the big jet and let one of the young pilots brings us down to the ranch so's we can have some fun."

By now my grandmother's Irish blood was boiling inside me and I was ready to drop loud mouth on his face. But airmanship has always come first, so I flexed my jaw muscles and eased the landing gear onto the Callahan.

As we taxied up to the ranch house, we were greeted by about ten or twelve bird dogs on the loose. They ran around with tongues hanging out, barking, wagging their tails, and in general making a big display of their joy. That pack of dogs knew that a hunt was coming up, and they were impatient to get started. The thought of a buzz job mixed with the sound of those yelping dogs caused my thoughts to drift to the spring of 1939 and Buster Higgins.

Buster never cared much for airplanes, but he would do anything for a bird dog. Buster was quite a bird hunter himself and owned seven dogs. Nancy was the oldest of Buster's dogs and had just presented him with a batch of speckled puppies.

Although Nancy was the best bird dog in those parts, Buster's favorite was a four-year-old named Little Elvie. On a hunting trip some time back, Little Elvie was shot by a deer hunter. A 30-06 slug passed through his body from shoulder to hip and produced a hole big enough to put a fist in. The blast broke numerous bones and ripped up his insides, enough to kill almost anything. But Little

Elvie, like Buster, was a tough one. He wasn't about to give up without a fight. After three days and nights of operations, transfusions, and prayers, Buster and the vet slowly pulled Little Elvie back from the edge of death. And there he was a year later, just a little stiff and very ornery. He was a watch dog now.

Little Elvie had Nancy's intelligence and Big Elvie's speed and strength. He had been a fine bird dog, but being shot changed all that. Now he would go after anything or anybody (except Buster), but his patched-up bones and muscles reduced his speed and agility. Little Elvie could only run with a limping three-legged gait and about half sideways. To adjust, he had learned to attack from the side or rear when his victim least expected it, and that's just how he got me.

I had landed my 1930 Model II Fleet airplane in Buster's pasture to see Nancy's new puppies, and for the fifth time to offer Buster his first airplane ride. After being turned down again, I went into my usual speech on how wonderful, safe, and practical flying could be for a man like Buster. Every time I gave that speech I got more eloquent. While lost in my eloquence, I leaned back against the board fence that separated us from the dogs and presented my tender backside to a four-inch-wide crack in the fencing. That was all Little Elvie needed.

I believe I reached the part about flying's overall safety record when Little Elvie's fangs catapulted me into the airspace. Needless to say, I lost all my eloquence. After throwing a couple of rocks and a few hastily chosen words at Little Elvie, I told Buster that I didn't give a tinker's toot if he ever got an airplane ride and roared off in the Fleet.

After going a few miles and failing to find a position that was comfortable to my offended parts, I boiled over. The thought of Buster doubled over with laughter at the seat of my pants hanging out was more than I could stand. Infuriated, I rolled the Fleet into a 180. I didn't know why I was going back, just that I was, and then I saw a familiar black Model A Ford bumping down the road.

"Buster's Model A," I said to myself.

I opened the throttle wide and the Kinner engine clattered up to the red line. The nose of the Fleet went down, and the wires began to scream as altitude was traded for airspeed. I leveled the Fleet inches above the road. The Model A and the Fleet were nose-to-nose and closing at 150 miles per hour. At the very last instant before getting a Ford emblem embossed in my spinner, I pulled back on the stick and the Fleet soared into a loop. My torn resting place ached with the G's.

At the top of the loop, I looked up at the road below and saw that the Model A had swerved into the ditch that paralleled the road. "Hot dog!" I shouted, and half rolled in an Immelmann. I could hardly wait to land to see if Buster was still laughing about my torn pants.

Throttling back, I slowed down, split S turn into final, lined up between the fences, and touched down on the road. I knew that Buster would need a pull to get his Model A out of the muddy ditch, so I tailed the Fleet around, jumped out with a big grin on my face, and left the engine running. As I approached Buster's Model A, it began to look like I had made a mistake, a bad mistake.

The two occupants of this Model A were pale and shaken. After I spent several minutes explaining how I had mistaken their Model A for someone else's and I extended my apologies, the pair recovered. Their shock rapidly grew into anger. One man took a little leather folder from his shirt pocket and presented it to me. The documents identified him as an agent of the Civil Aeronautics Administration. The enormous magnitude of my mistake dawned on me, and their anger grew more intense.

I figured that they would get everything that Little Elvie missed. They were shouting, waving their hands, and calling me an aerial maniac. I was displaying my shredded rear and explaining how I was not responsible for my actions because I was the victim of a sneak attack by a mad dog. At the height of this confusion, Buster drove up in his Model A.

Buster stood back for several minutes and listened to the three of us shout at each other about Civil Air Regulations, airmanship, and my bloody bottom. Then he stepped up and introduced himself.

Suddenly, like flying out of a boiling dark cloud into smooth sunlight, the conversation shifted to bird hunting and bird dogs. The CAA men even called Buster "Mr. Higgins." It became clear that they were avid bird hunters and that Buster's and Nancy's reputations had spread all the way to San Antonio. Upon hearing of Nancy's puppies, they had driven all the way out to Buster's place in the hope of buying one of the puppies. Now Buster didn't have much schooling, but like a bird dog sniffing out a quail, he got the drift of things real quick. He knew that I was in trouble, and I guess he figured he was indebted for Little Elvie's inhospitable act.

In his slow reassuring way, Buster rambled on for long minutes about Nancy's puppies and how pretty they were. Then, mixing bird dog talk with my problem, he explained that I was his neighbor and good friend. He closed by telling the CAA men that their long drive from San Antonio was wasted because he had sold the last puppy to me that very morning. Actually, he hadn't sold any of them, but he gave me a stick and rudder to maneuver with.

I wasted no time in explaining how I was not a bird hunter and that it would be a waste of talent for that dog to lie around my hangar all day with nothing to do but chase butterflies. Telling my lie with conviction, I explained that I only paid $20.00 for him and would be glad to sell him for that if I could just get in my Fleet and get out of there because the engine was still running. Well, it was very quiet for a long time as the two CAA men and I straight-faced each other like players in a poker game. Then, slowly, one of them reached into his pocket and said, "O.K., mister, here's your twenty dollars, but don't ever let me catch you below five hundred feet again."

I was in the Fleet and gone faster than Little Elvie had ripped the seat out of my pants. Later on, Buster got the money, they got a good bird dog, I didn't hear a thing from San Antonio, and that was that.

Back at the Callahan, my four passengers had their gear unloaded and were walking toward Shorty's pickup with yapping bird dogs swirling around them. I had the Aztec lined up for take-off and brought the power up full. The wheels eased off the Callahan, and the thought of Loud Mouth returned to rekindle old fires deep inside me. "All of us old Longhorns aren't as useless as you think," I muttered toward Loud Mouth. Leaving the power at max, the Aztec roared past the hunters and attracted their attention. Lightly loaded and with excess power and speed, I pulled the Aztec into near vertical flight and zoomed a thousand feet upward. At the top, near zero airspeed, I performed a hammerhead to the left. Screaming vertically downward, I had Loud Mouth squarely in my sights. I could see him looking up at me—pale, mouth open, and frozen in his tracks. "This one is for Shorty," I grimaced as I leveled the Aztec just above their heads. Zooming north toward Dallas, I had loud mouth out of my system, but I shifted uncomfortably in my seat as I remembered Little Elvie.

FUNDAMENTALS

IT WAS DRY AND HOT IN 1933. MATTERS WERE BAD AND getting worse because the worst drought in Texas history was in the making. The land on which we depended became more and more barren. It seemed that my flying lessons were also becoming more and more barren. I was confined to the front cockpit and required to repeat the same lesson over and over: climb, descend, turn, straight and level, stall.

Bo insisted that I take the front cockpit with its bare instrument panel, saying, "Fly by attitude! Fly by feel! Fly by sound! Feel your airplane. Listen to your airplane. It's telling you things." With only that to direct and encourage me, we repeated the same maneuvers over and over.

Drill, drill, and drill; over and over we repeated the routine. It was as relentless as the drought. The only relief was on landing, when Bo would allow me to make a 180- or 360-degree power-off approach to landing.

The drills continued. I was paying for each lesson and wanted to learn quickly, but my patience was growing as short as my savings. Both would run out soon. Trying to indicate my unhappiness to Bo, I asked, "Why are we doing the same things over and over?"

"Well, boy, if you wanted to be a baseball player, there are four things that you would have to do real good. They are: run, bat, throw, and catch. Those are the fundamentals of baseball. The things we're doing are the fundamentals of flight. That's all you can do with an airplane. Everything else is just some combination of these fundamentals. To be a good pilot, you've got to do them good, and you've got to do them without really thinking about what you're doing."

Knowing full well that *real* flying involved reading all manner of instruments, throwing switches, twisting knobs, and pushing buttons, I asked, "Well, why can't I do them just as well from the rear cockpit?"

Bo quickly harpooned my concept of *real* flying by answering, "Because of all them gauges! If I put you in the rear cockpit, you'll start reading them gauges and the next thing we know them gauges will be telling you how to fly the airplane, rather than you telling the airplane how to fly."

I accepted his explanation and made a sincere effort to master the five fundamentals without benefit of flight instruments.

"Straight and level! Get your nose up, boy. You're losing altitude. Listen to those wires. You're going too fast. Get your nose up. Pick a spot on the horizon. Keep her straight."

"Climb. Get your nose down. You can't force this airplane to climb. Still too high. Get it down for the best climb speed. Listen to those wires. Right rudder. Right rudder. Keep her straight."

"Turn, Rudder and stick. Rudder and stick. Get them together. Hold the bank steady. Use the horizon. Get your nose up. You're losing altitude."

"Stall. Rudder. Rudder. Keep her straight. Wings level. Pick up that low wing. More rudder. Feel that yaw. Nose higher. There's the stall. Nose down. Power up. Nose up. Wings level."

"Descend. You're diving, boy! Listen to those wires. You're too fast. Get the nose up. Slow her down. Keep her straight. O.k., now! Power up and back to straight and level."

On and on the training continued until I felt that I had mastered all five fundamental maneuvers without flight instruments. But the drills went on. I was growing more distressed with Bo and had reached the point where enough was enough. As we walked toward the airplane for my next lesson, I asked, "What are we going to do today?"

Bo's matter-of-fact reply came. "Practice fundamentals."

I stopped and angrily said, "Bo, I've had enough of these fundamentals. I'm good enough now. It's time for me to move on to something else in flying."

Shocked by my challenge to his right to determine what should be taught and for how long, Bo swelled slightly as his temper was fused. Looking angrily at me with a firmly set jaw, his face reddened slightly, and his stern eyes penetrated and dominated every part of my body and soul.

He spoke slowly and with great intensity: "You listen to me, boy. When you can do the fundamentals with your right arm tied down and your eyes blindfolded, then you're good enough. When you can fly the airplane without gauges in the driving rain, with engines on fire and parts falling off, with passengers screaming and puking, then you're good enough. When things are so bad that there's no way in the world for the airplane to fly, but you can fly it, then you're good enough. You'll be good enough when I say you're good enough because I'm the only one that'll know when you're that good. You just keep your mouth shut and show me some good, tough flying!"

Stunned into silence, I realized that Bo wasn't teaching me to fly for today. He was working on tomorrow's tomorrows. With renewed respect for my teacher, I quietly mounted the instrumentless front cockpit and awaited his commands.

"Climb! Descend! Turn! Straight and level! Stall!"

THE
LAST
MISSION

G ENTLEMEN, YOUR TARGET FOR TODAY IS . . ." THE
briefing officer began. The tip of his long and thin pointer
rested on a distant point in Germany. The zigzag courses
to and from the target were marked with black tape that stretched
more than halfway across the huge map on the briefing room wall.
The courses had been laid out by the mission planners at Headquarters.

Combat aircrews didn't like mission planners. Although the
planners knew nothing of when or where the Germans might
relocate their defenses, they always told us that they would guide
us around known fighter and flak concentrations. The mission
planners—who never saw a wing blown off a B-17 by antiaircraft
fire or witnessed a friend take a 20mm shell in the chest—even
thought that their devious courses could surprise the Germans.

Imagine surprising them with an armada of 200 to 300 bombers,
heavily loaded with bombs, fuel, men, guns, and ammo, trudging
along at 180 miles per hour. Imagine surprising those who flew

fighters at speeds of 400 miles per hour. Imagine surprising those who fired the dreaded 88, a radar-guided cannon that could hurl 40 pounds of exploding steel five miles high.

We were not misled. There were few surprises in heavy bombardment. The enemy knew when we were coming, and we knew what they would do to stop us.

On some missions, we faced as many as 250 fighters, attacking in groups of 30 or 40 airplanes, firing machine guns, cannons, and rockets. Those firing machine guns had to arc in close enough to drive their bullets home. We could shoot back at them, and that made us feel a little better, but those firing cannons and rockets could stay safely outside the effective range of our fifty-caliber machine guns.

Some enemy fighters had side-firing rocket launchers. They would fly parallel to the formation, just beyond the range of our guns, and lob rocket after rocket at us. They would fly alongside, firing at will, for as long as an hour, or until their rocket supply was gone.

Beginning at the outer edges of the formation (the "coffin corners"), they could slowly blast their way inward and obliterate an entire bomb group and its 200 or so crewmen. The only defense against them was a fighter escort. If we had fighter support, our guys could shoot them down or drive them away. Without fighters, you simply held onto your lucky charm and prayed.

Five miles over Germany, prayer and lucky charms were all we had. There was no place to hide. There were no foxholes, no trees or rocks to get behind, not even a flat earth to squeeze against when the shooting started. You tensed into as small a space as possible, hoped that harm would somehow bounce off your tightly flexed muscles, and tried to do your job.

At important targets, the fighter defenses were supported by 200 or more antiaircraft cannons. The men firing the cannons loved those neatly arranged courses that our mission planners laid out. Those straight lines, followed so expertly by our well-trained navigators, leading directly to the target, were murder. The last 40 miles to the target, where no deviations in altitude, heading, or airspeed were allowed, were called "Purple Heart Alley."

Many enemy radar eyes followed the bombers up the Alley. Radar could determine a bomber's altitude within a few feet, its speed within a few feet per second, and its heading within a fraction of a degree. With this information, a computer would make the necessary calculations to set the altitude-sensitive detonator, determine the lead angle, point the gun toward the bomber's projected position, and fire. The intersection of flight path and trajectory was assured. It was all very scientific and very deadly.

A good fighter escort could drive off the enemy's airborne defenses, but nothing could be done about the flak. You flew the airplane and hoped they missed.

The difference between being hit or being missed by a flak shell was mostly a matter of luck—or Providence perhaps. Survival in a flak storm often depended on the wind currents along the five-mile trajectory from the ground to a bomber's position. Unseen by the German radar and unknown to the computer, these wind currents could push the death shells off their well-calculated path. Later on, the Germans learned to gang thirty or forty guns to one radar and fire them simultaneously to compensate for wind uncertainties; thus creating a "flak box" that surrounded a bomber.

If your ship was selected by the radar operator as the center of the box, it was all over. The very best you could hope for was minor injuries, a bailout, and admission to a German prison hospital; the worst—well, we never considered the worst, but great losses were an accepted fact of life (or death) at places like Munster, Schweinfurt, Ploesti, and Berlin.

Not all missions were that deadly. There were a few attacks on lightly guarded targets where no losses were suffered. They were called "milk runs." Regardless of the target, though, two missions were feared simply because of their number: the thirteenth (the unlucky one) and the fiftieth (the last one). Few men made it to their last mission. Apart from those who lost their lives along the way, an even greater number returned to the states with injuries serious enough to end their flying. Some just cracked under the pressure and were assigned other duties.

For the few that made it through the first forty-nine missions, the thing foremost in their minds was the lives lost on the fiftieth mission. After each mission, we expected sad news like, "Well, Tom (or Bill or Joe) so-and-so got it today," but the one that tore at you and lingered in the memory was when they added, "...and it was his last mission." Somehow, that made it worse, even if the man was from another squadron or a total stranger. It was worse because he could have gone home to laugh and live in safety if he had just made it through his last mission. But he didn't. Instead, he would remain forever one mission, and an ocean's span, from home.

Men responded differently to the pressure of the last mission. Some were quiet, withdrawn, even hostile, and imagined they could beat the odds by sheer determination. A few succeeded in postponing the last mission by various illnesses. When their names were posted for their last mission, they would be seriously ill and incapable of flying. They would have fever or chills or diarrhea or vomiting or various combined ailments. These men were not cowards; they proved that by completing forty-nine missions. Their illnesses were not faked, they were real. Dreading the last mission jinx was so great that it manifested itself in genuine physical disabilities.

Others faced the last mission with a great deal of laughing, shouting, and bragging. They tried to laugh away the last mission jinx as something ridiculous or nonexistent. Some bragged about close calls on earlier missions, loudly claimed they would beat the odds, and shouted their defiance of the jinx. They desperately tried to conceal their fear behind a brash exterior, but make no mistake, they all lived with gnawing, agonizing, consuming fear; we all did.

I had completed forty-eight missions and the odds were closing in on me; I was worried. My copilot, Bill Jackson, had joined me on my thirteenth mission as a fresh replacement from the states. He had started his career as a wide-eyed and frightened second lieutenant, ready to turn back from the target for any reason. He was a different man now. With thirty-six missions to his credit, he had developed into a capable pilot and a brave fighting man. We grew as close as men dare in combat, but rarely exposed our deepest feelings to each other. However, I knew that our crew would soon be alerted for another mission, and I needed to talk to someone about the fears growing in me as mission no. 50 approached. An opportunity presented itself one evening while we were relaxing outside the mess hall.

We were gazing at "Danny's Dream," an F model B-17 with nine missions to its credit. There was a well-endowed, auburn-haired nude painted on the nose. The discreetly posed beauty had the words "Danny's Dream" circling her well-rounded bottom. Danny and most of his crew died on our last trip to Berlin. Although severely wounded, Danny's copilot managed to fly "Danny's Dream" home safely. He was awarded the Distinguished Flying Cross for saving some of his crew and the airplane.

Our B-17 had been battered into submission on the same trip. It limped home, but collapsed and died shortly after landing. We were a crew without a ship, and "Danny's Dream" was a ship without a crew. "Danny's Dream" was ours now.

As we watched our new ship resting in the distance, our casual conversation drifted loosely from one pleasant subject to another. We always avoided talk of the war and our terrible misgivings about our safety, but this evening seemed different. The sun, reddened and dimmed by faraway clouds, slowly ended its day in the west. Gradually, a cold, gray fog was drawn from the darkened east to fill the vacant sky. The fog silently crept across the channel to blanket the base and create a chilling loneliness that magnified our fears and drew us together.

"Look at that, Bill! She's just going to sit there and be swallowed by that fog," I said. Bill Jackson was silently watching our Fortress disappear into the mist.

The night darkened. The fog grew damp and dense. I added, "You can barely make her out now." His only answer was a slow, soft grunt that indicated agreement.

"Old Danny let her get all bumped and bruised, but she's a darn good ship."

Bill grunted more agreement and added, "Yeah, but it's the crew that counts, and ours is a great crew."

"Yeah, each one is a great guy, but they're peculiar as a crew," I observed.

"What do you mean by that?"

"Well, they never trained together as a crew. As a crew, they just happened. We started out last year with a bunch of volunteers from the ground crews when we were short on aircrews. Most of them didn't even know how to get in the airplane, let alone operate it. And we've had a steady stream of replacements."

"Yes, we've had our share of the losses. Tubbs is the last original volunteer. He came on board the same time I did—your thirteenth, remember?"

"Do I ever. Before he volunteered to fly right waist, Tubbs worked in the motor pool. He was driving a staff car when I came over from the states. He learned his gunnery by trial and error."

Bill seemed proud of Tubbs' achievements and said, "Yeah, and he's pretty good. He's got some good hits on enemy fighters."

"Right," I agreed, "but he just doesn't look the part. He's more than just a little plump—the guys don't call him Tubby because his name is Tubbs. And you know how he's always going out of his way to listen to our gripes and help everybody with their problems. He's worse than some chaplains I've seen—all that's great and I'm glad to have him on my crew. What I mean is, he just don't look like a gunner."

Bill thought quietly about my description of Tubbs but had nothing to say, so I added, "And you've heard about those lucky socks of his, haven't you? He puts them on before each mission and takes them off when we get back. He says that's what gets him through. Rogers told me that he never washes them and won't wash them until his fifty missions are over."

"Yeah, that's right. Tubbs has those lucky socks, but he isn't any worse than the rest of us. Rogers always puts on that red and black garter he got from a dancer in London. He wouldn't fly a mission without it. And me, I've got my St. Christopher medal. All of us have something to get us through. Don't you?"

I was set back by his simple and direct question. I had no lucky charm, but the surprise was in realizing that I never felt the need for one. A little embarrassed that I might be different from the others, I shook my head and motioned his attention back toward our ship. "You're going to get this whole wacky crew when she becomes yours."

His gaze drifted from the fog-shrouded B-17 back to me, and he quietly said, "No, she won't ever be mine."

I reminded him that I would be going home soon. "Come on, Bill, they'll make you aircraft commander when I'm gone. You know I've only got two missions to go."

"Yes, I know. How do you feel about it?"

"I'm not sure, Bill. I'm beginning to worry about the odds catching up with me."

I was reluctant to get directly into a description of my rising fears, so I redirected the conversation. "I'm a little worried about what's going to happen to the crew."

"Some of the guys have been talking about it."

"What have they said?"

"Oh, not a whole lot. Rogers said that if they change up the crew assignments, he would like to get into something besides the ball turret."

"I mean what have they said about me and my last mission?"

"Well-l-l-l." He was reluctant.

I smiled a coaxing smile and encouraged, "Come on, Bill."

"Well, they're all wondering how you are going to react if your last one is a real bad one. Most of them think you're going to do the tough-guy act and try to scare away any harm."

"What do you think, Bill?"

"I don't think you have a thing to worry about. You're going to get through this war without a scratch. You've got it made."

There was a calm conviction in his words that struck me silent. I studied the seriousness in his eyes for a minute, and then I tried to tell him I was frightened without actually confessing it.

"It would be a lot easier to make it if that were true, but we won't know if I've got it made until number fifty is over."

He responded calmly. "No, sir, I know it right now."

"What do you mean?"

He didn't answer right away and was laboring under deep-rooted emotions when he did. "Captain, you don't need a lucky charm. It probably never occurred to you to have one. It wouldn't occur to you because you're already protected from harm."

A surprised look must have flashed across my face because he went on to explain, "You know I'm a Catholic, and to us Catholics the Virgin Mary holds a place of high honor. Just think about her. Of all the women in the world, she was the purest. She was the one selected by God to bear His son. I love her as much as I do our Savior. Well, I have this belief about how the Virgin Mother protects some men."

"I believe she travels with them, hovers around them, and when danger threatens, she holds them in her arms just like she did Jesus. A man held in her arms can't be hurt. He can't be touched." He paused, breathed a quiet breath, and then with a simple openness of heart that amplified his sincerity added, "Captain, you're one of those men."

I was astounded. It took some time for me to regain myself and attempt to brush away his words. "Now wait a minute, Bill. I've been awful lucky, but...."

He cut me off. "Lucky! Captain, that isn't luck. Look at yourself the way I have. I have studied you. You've flown forty-eight missions. I've been on thirty-six of them with you, and most of them were pretty darn rough. We've been through the meat grinder time and time again. We've flown with hydraulics out, with electricals out, and engines out. We've flown with airplanes on fire. We've brought some birds home shot so full of holes that they really shouldn't have stayed in the air, but somehow they did. And we've seen a lot of good men die in those airplanes. But just look at yourself. You don't even have a Purple Heart. You haven't been scratched. You've got the Good Mother's arms around you all right. You're protected.''

Normally, I would have poked fun at anyone making a statement like that. To me, it sounded a lot like Tubbs' lucky socks. But Bill Jackson made it seem real, made it seem true, and I wanted to believe it. Then a rebuttal arose in my mind and burst out. ''Maybe you're protected and it just spilled over on me. I ain't never been religious like you. You'd be the one, not me.''

''No, you're the one, Captain. I've stayed close to you hoping to be shielded by your protection. You're my lucky socks. That's why I turned down the chance to have my own plane and crew last month. I want to get out of this war alive, and I figure my best chance is in staying close to you.''

''But after my last mission, what then, Bill?''

''I'm not sure, Captain. I'm worried and scared. You have no cause for things like that. You'll make it. I'm not sure if I will. I'm scared, Captain. I'm scared stiff.''

Not since his early missions had I seen such fear expressed in his wide eyes. His frank confession rushed over me like an ocean wave. The fear that I had felt ebbed away as I realized the depth of his concern. I was stunned by this reversal of feeling between us and, for a moment, I sat speechless. In an effort to put him at ease again, I quoted the old cliche, ''There's nothing wrong in being afraid, Bill. We all are.''

My hollow words seemed to have no effect as he nervously wrung his hands. Fear is a lonesome, personal thing that resists help from the outside. Each man must fight his own battle against fear. Embarrassed by my inability to help him, I tried to lighten the conversation. ''Aw, Bill, we've got nothing to worry about. You know what's going to happen to us?''

He sat gazing at our battle-scarred Fortress. I poked him in the ribs with my elbow and repeated, ''Come on, you know what's going to happen to us?''

Embarrassed by his confession, he finally managed a difficult, ''What?''

''When this thing is over, we're all going home. And when we get old and gray, we'll have a big reunion and laugh about this whole mess.'' From there the conversation dissolved into chatter about home, jobs, girls, marriage, and kids with braces on their teeth. We sat side-by-side in the damp fog, enjoying the warmth of our friendship until it was very late.

The weather worsened. Low ceilings, rain, and more fog moved in the next day. Poor flying conditions persisted for almost a week as a warm front stood stagnant over most of Europe. We enjoyed those days playing, laughing, relaxing, but always remembering the terrible job ahead when the weather improved. The aircrews wished the bad weather would last forever; it put our war on hold. Weather removed us from danger, but we knew it was only temporary. When it cleared, our crew was one of the first to be posted on the Alert List.

As the briefing officer guided his long black pointer across the map, our eyes followed the zigzag courseline to the target. We were to bomb the synthetic oil plant at Magdeburg in central Germany. The plant was producing about 1,000 gallons of synthetic oil per day for German war machines. Much of it went into German fighters. At the time, we thought that knocking out the plant would deprive German fighters of their much-needed oil, and thus help our own cause. We learned later, however, that we were assisting the land war that was to begin soon at Normandy.

We were to fly east out of England over the Netherlands in an apparent direct attack on Hamburg. Just short of Hamburg, we would turn southeast and fly up the Elbe River in an apparent attack on Berlin. About fifty miles from Berlin, the Elbe turns abruptly south; we would make that turn also. That would leave a fifty-mile dash to Magdeburg on the west bank of the Elbe. After the strike, we would return directly to England. We would fly about 580 miles going in and about 480 miles coming out.

Unlike the missions we flew in early 1943 when our P-47s could take us only about 200 miles, the new P-51B's, equipped with external fuel tanks, could stay with us for the entire mission. Fighter coverage would be a blessing. They would keep enemy fighters occupied and off our backs. Although we would still have to face the radar-guided flak at the target, there was a good chance that this mission might be an easy one. Good fighter protection could prevent the massive fighter assaults we had seen in the past. Then, if we did surprise the defenders at Magdeburg or if they had but a few antiaircraft cannons, we might sail through this with few losses.

All of these thoughts reeled through my mind as we prepared for take-off. My palms were sweaty. My mouth was dry. I kept repeating the statements made by the briefing officer: "Our fake attacks on Hamburg and Berlin will dilute their defenses. Our fighters will totally occupy the fighter defenses they send up." I repeated them over and over and hoped they were true.

I began to understand the reactions of other men to their last mission. I shared their fear. Then in a flash of guilt, I remembered that this was only my forty-ninth, and not my last, mission. As I taxied into position for take-off, I thought of Bill Jackson and the Virgin Mary. I thought of Danny and the auburn-haired beauty on the nose. I thought of Tubbs and his lucky socks. I tried to think of anything that would take my mind off the danger ahead. Then it was our turn for take-off. I inhaled fully and exhaled completely to relieve the tension; then I pushed the throttles full open. It had begun.

The frontal system that cleared out the bad weather left a cool, clear morning with unlimited visibility. The stars still sparkled against the awakening sky. It was like the well-remembered days of my boyhood when zestful antics in an open-cockpit biplane were the most important thing in my life. It was a day for flying and enjoying, not for making war. The peaceful beauty surrounding me blended with the reassuring drone of our four smooth-running radial engines. The English countryside fell below and behind our climbout.

In its high place, the thin cirrus clouds glowed faintly orange as the red-orange fingers of the yet unrisen sun streaked across the sky. The air was crisp and clean smelling. This was a day to fly and enjoy the early morning sky halfway between starlight and sunlight. This was a day to fly and enjoy the rich greens and browns of a springtime earth. Everything above, around, and below seemed naturally clean, orderly, and at peace.

Like an enraptured student pilot rising above the flat plane of the earth for the first time, I was totally captured by the magical blending of land, sea, sky, and air. I was drawn away from my thoughts of the certain danger we faced. For a moment, there was nothing but my soaring spirit, blended with a smooth flying machine, adrift in a close approach to heaven. Then, abruptly, another Fortress slid into formation on my left. I was reawakened to the grim business at hand. The formation was amassing. Our group put up 17 airplanes. Joining with 15 other bomb groups from other bases, we would be a formation of 290 Fortresses.

While there may be strength in numbers, there is little comfort in them. The mission planners always sent a large number of bombers when they expected great losses. The object was to get enough bombers over the target to do the job. The tougher the target, the more they would send. A formation of 290 bombers was our first hint that things might not go as smoothly as planned.

The discomfort we felt because of the large number of bombers, and the grim message it usually implied, was quickly eased when our fighter escort appeared on time, high above us, at mid-channel. Other than seeing the home base (which means making it home safely), the most beautiful sight to a bomber crew is a fighter escort; and our escort of 109 fighters was gorgeous.

Each P-51B was sleek and powerful, shiny and fast. The fat fuel tanks tucked under each wing marred their natural beauty, but we were quick to overlook that blemish to their graceful lines. External fuel tanks were one thing that allowed them to go the distance with us. The other thing was their greatly reduced speed. We were in clumsy, slow airplanes going as fast as we could. The fighter pilots were in nimble, fast airplanes going as slowly as they dared. They made their take-off and early portion of the climb on internal fuel. Switching to external fuel would refill the internal tanks and provide fuel for the balance of the climb and some cruise. After about two hours, the external fuel would be exhausted and the empty tanks jettisoned. This would place our streamlined, fully armed Mustang escort high above Hamburg with maximum internal fuel.

"What an advantage," I thought. If German fighters took off at Hamburg, Berlin, or Magdeburg on short notice to intercept us, they would be denied the use of external fuel to facilitate a rapid climb to our 28,000 feet. If the enemy sent fighters without external fuel to our altitude, they would arrive with most of their internal fuel exhausted. They would be limited to only a few minutes of combat. I was beginning to feel good about this mission as the full disk of the sun emerged above the distant horizon. Amsterdam was just ahead.

Miles below, the Zuider Zee was a small disk that glistened. As I watched its rippling surface reflect the slanting rays of early morning sunlight, it drew me into a trancelike spell. My thoughts went back to the early-morning events that saddled our ship with command responsibility. Our group was designated the Lead Group for this mission. Colonel Austin, our group commander, was named the Mission Commander. Some mission commanders flew their own ships on the mission they commanded, but Colonel Austin felt that command was a responsibility requiring his full attention, and should not be subordinated to pilot duties. He always selected one bomber for a "command ship." For this mission, he had chosen our ship.

A jump seat was rigged near Ron Bailey's station at the radios. From there, Colonel Austin would make observations, receive information, and make the important decisions affecting the mission. The whole thing seemed unbelievable, and I welcomed the spell cast by the Zuider Zee.

I drifted into a dream world of no bombers, no fighters, and no flak. Unblinking, I stared with wide eyes at its magical surface and willingly submitted to its hypnotic powers. I welcomed those few minutes of escape from the reality that lay ahead. Then it slowly slid from my view beneath the wing of "Danny's Dream," and the spell was broken. The roar of engines, the subfreezing cold of 28,000 feet, and the rubbery taste of oxygen supplied by my mask returned to my awareness.

I looked at Bill Jackson. His rosary was wrapped around his heavily gloved left hand; he gripped the cross in his palm. I could see his jaw moving behind his oxygen mask as he recited a prayer.

The things he had told me a week before as we sat outside the mess hall came to mind. I thought about the Virgin Mary. She was like a stranger to me. Years earlier, I was taught that she was the mother of Jesus Christ. Beyond that, she was but a vague figure recalled from boyhood images formed by pictures and statues on the fringe of my Protestant upbringing. "Why would she single me out?" I questioned, and quickly answered, "Aw, that's just Bill Jackson. He's been getting more and more religious all the time."

I looked again at my copilot. He seemed to have finished his prayer. Reaching across the short distance between our seats, I punched him on the shoulder. He looked at me with a smile visible from behind his oxygen mask. I winked a reassuring wink and his smile got bigger. I thought, "Bill Jackson is the best darn copilot in the Army." Having a man like him with me made me feel comfortable, even secure.

Then reality came rasping through my imagined security on the mission frequency. From somewhere ahead in the bomber stream, we heard those dreaded words repeated: "Enemy fighters at twelve o'clock. Enemy fighters at twelve o'clock."

The voice was distant and tinny; it sounded artificial and unbelievable. There had to be some mistake. We weren't even out of the Netherlands yet. We had not crossed over into Germany. Looking back, we could still see Amsterdam and the North Sea beyond. Never had the Germans committed their fighters so early; there had to be some mistake. But the mission frequency was alive with reports from men in the front echelon several miles ahead of us. The reports identified Me-109s and Fw-190s, totaling perhaps 200 fighters.

Looking up, I saw our P-51's external fuel tanks dropping and the fighters accelerating to combat speed. An enormous battle involving 300 fighters developed above us. Twisting, turning, climbing, and diving in offensive and defensive maneuvers, the fighters crisscrossed the sky with white entwined contrails that glistened against the vivid blue. From our close-up vantage point, we watched in disbelief as the German fighters avoided our bombers and attacked our fighters. Not one bomber was touched by enemy fire.

Our guys were outnumbered by two to one as the battle raged. We could see some of our escort pilots parachuting away from their burning planes. Some could be seen trailing smoke, and turning back toward England trying to guide their damaged airplane home to safety. But our guys and our airplanes were better than theirs, and many of the Germans were blasted from the sky. Then as suddenly as they had appeared, the Germans abruptly disengaged and sped away in unison. Forced to stay with our formation, our fighters could not give chase.

The quiet sky was ours again. There was time to assess the damage and its effect on the mission. Although the battle was brief—it had lasted no more than ten minutes—we had lost fourteen Mustangs. The Germans had lost thirty or more fighters, but it was a German victory. They had forced our fighters to jettison their external fuel tanks and precious fuel. They had forced our Mustangs to use internal fuel at the enormously high fuel consumption rates of combat and war emergency power settings. They had forced most of our escort to use much of their ammunition.

Reporting to Colonel Austin, the fighter leader estimated that they had enough fuel to accompany us for only another fifty miles. Just short of Hamburg, they would have to break off and return to England to refuel and rearm. On the mission frequency, I heard the fighter leader tell Colonel Austin, "If you decide to continue the mission, Colonel, we well refuel and proceed toward the target along your withdrawal route. We should rendezvous with your formation about halfway home."

Those words struck us like a bucket of ice water. Cold chills rippled across my skin. I was well acquainted with Colonel Robert Howell Austin. We often joked that his real name was "Rock Hard" and that Robert Howell was an alias. Colonel Austin was a hard-nosed, ramrod-straight, by-the-book West Pointer. To him, a mission assignment was like a direct order from General Eisenhower at Supreme Allied Headquarters: a do-or-die commitment. I knew there would be no turning back. Colonel Austin's stiff, measured voice said, "Thank you, Major. You know the assigned altitude for the withdrawal. We will rendezvous at your earliest convenience." A collective gasp came from the 2,900 men in the formation.

The German plan was now clear and seemed to be working. From radar sites along the French and Dutch coasts, they had observed our take-off and climb. It took more than one hour for our bombers and fighters to get into the air and form up before heading an course. This gave the Germans time to assemble the fighter force that met us and stripped us of our escort. I tried not to imagine what other things these clever Germans had planned, but I couldn't prevent my mind from racing ahead.

We would overreach our fighter support by a substantial distance and time. We were striking a target of great importance to the Wehrmacht. They would do their best to beat back our attack before we reached Magdeburg. For those of us that did reach Magdeburg, there would be thick swarms of deadly flak to plow through. Those who survived the nightmare of the drop zone and headed home would be severely punished by the Luftwaffe. There would be no relief until we met our fighters about halfway between Magdeburg and England. We were going to pay a high price to deprive the Germans of a little oil. I scowled at the mission planners, who were carefully plotting our progress in the safety of the war room at headquarters. I wished they had to fly this mission with us.

The fifty miles disappeared quickly. Through the crystalline sky ahead and below, we could see Hamburg awakening to a beautiful morning. Families were rising, eating breakfast, and preparing for school and work. The kids would go to school, where they would be told of their great leader, Adolf Hitler. The parents would go to work to make the weapons of war.

I was angered by this visualization and thought to myself, "If I were mission commander, I would bomb Hamburg as a target of opportunity and return to England with our fighters." Quick to justify my command decision, I reasoned, "We would get an important target and save many lives. It's the most reasonable and safest thing to do."

Words from the fighter leader interrupted my fantasy. "Big Hawk One, this is Little Bird One. It's time for us to return to the nest."

"Roger, Little Bird. Your withdrawal is approved," was Colonel Austin's only reply. Everyone listening on the mission frequency hung for long, silent moments expecting more, perhaps a "Thanks" or even a "Thanks, and good luck," but there was only silence and finality to be heard. Even the fighter pilots were expecting more because, instead of peeling off and reversing course toward England, they hung in tight formation. Several miles had slid behind us when the silence was broken by the fighter leader. With a compassion shared only by combat air crewmen who had lived through aerial warfare and knew what we were going to face, he soberly said, "Good luck, you guys." Then squadron by squadron the fighters rolled out of formation and disappeared. We were alone.

When we were almost over Hamburg, the formation turned southeast up the Elbe River. The heart of Hitler's hate was squarely in front of us. "Will they accept our fake attack and rush their defenses to Berlin while we turn toward Magdeburg?" My question was a wish, a hope, more than a real question. But the wish was inconsistent with the two important facts that had already emerged on this mission. One, the Germans somehow correctly reasoned that we would travel many miles into Germany, so they had stripped us of our fighters early in the mission. Two, they were not fooled by our fake attack on Hamburg. Not one fighter or flak shell was seen there. They were allowing us to trudge deeper and deeper into their trap. Then my mind recoiled with a dreadful thought. "There has been a security leak! They know we're going to Magdeburg!"

It had happened before with disastrous results. Given advance knowledge of the target, the direction of the attack, and the altitude, the enemy had massive fighter and antiaircraft defenses in place and waiting. The carnage was unbelievable.

My strong impulse was to pick up the mike, tell Colonel Austin of my discovery, and recommend that we abort the mission. I grabbed the mike and fingered the intercom button. Pausing, I realized that my imagination was running rampant and slowly returned the mike to its holder.

The long missions were the most difficult because they gave the imagination time to work. Droning unresisted, hour after hour, with the autopilot flying the airplane, there was nothing to do but think of what lay ahead. There was only imagination and no reality. Most veteran air crewmen welcomed the first fighter pass or the first flak burst because then there was only reality and no imagination. "God, why doesn't somebody shoot at us?" I silently pleaded.

No shots were fired. We were within fifty miles of Berlin and the Elbe could be seen swinging southward toward Magdeburg. As we made the turn to the south, I was convinced that the Germans knew from the start that the target was Magdeburg and that we would approach from the north. They probably even knew the final assault altitude. Otherwise, they would not let us get so close to Berlin and Hitler. Had our fake attack worked, the sky near Berlin would be swarming with fighters. The vacant and silent sky around us signaled danger. Now, imagination and reality began to merge. The worst you could imagine was about to happen because they knew we were coming.

The Germans introduced a new defensive tactic at Magdeburg. In addition to approximately 300 enemy fighters that met us forty miles north of Magdeburg, there were twin-engined aircraft— Messerschmitt 110s—cruising about 5,000 feet above us. At first, we were curious about their unusual position. We guessed that they were photo ships positioned to film the battle. To our horror, we discovered that each was equipped with four machine guns mounted vertically in the fuselage. Flying just above the reach of our gravity-restrained return fire, flying straight and level, they could fire directly down upon us without maneuvering. We were locked on the bomb run, and with altitude, airspeed, and heading held constant by the bombsight-directed autopilot, the Me-110s had no trouble positioning themselves to rain bullets on the bombers. There was no place to turn, no place to duck, no place to hide.

A death rain poured down. The only letup came when other enemy aircraft zoomed in close enough to be endangered by the bullets.

The enemy's fighter attacks were coordinated by someone in the overhead aircraft. Each Me-110 controlled three groups of ten to twelve fighters. One group would be called in to attack from the left. Within seconds, the second group would be signaled to attack from the right, followed by the third group attacking from below. The overhead machine gunner stopped only long enough for each group of his fighters to pass by the bomber. Within a minute or less, a bomber would be hit by thousands of bullets and cannon shells from about thirty to thirty-six fighters.

There was no way to effectively defend ourselves from such a highly concentrated attack; it was devastating. Either all on board would be killed and ride their spiraling Fortress to earth, or the enemy would get a solid hit in the fuel tanks or bomb load and the plane would explode.

If there was any good in this, it was in the low number of overhead aircraft—there were only ten of them. Because attacks of this type were so acutely focused, they had to select one bomber at a time. With 290 of us and only ten Me-110s, the odds against selection for attack were pretty good. However, if your bomber was selected, the odds of escaping were zero. Although we took light machine-gun fire from German fighters passing quickly on their way to regroup for one of the concentrated attacks on other bombers, we were doing well and within thirty miles of bomb release. The bay doors were open. Herb Tollison and his bombsight were flying the ship.

During the bombing run, a pilot has little to do. I tried to sit quietly, hands in lap, not acting nervous. I occupied the time by helping the gunners scan the sky in search of the enemy, and the enemy was there. Helplessly, we watched as one of the Me-110s maneuvered above the bomber directly in front of us. Two thousand yards ahead, we witnessed the devastating attack destroy the bomber in less than two minutes.

As the bullets rained from above, the fighter groups attacked from left, from right, and from below. The bomber quivered, seemed to falter, and began breaking up. The right wing buckled, spraying its high-octane gasoline across its fuselage. As the bomber rolled to its right, an enormous fireball engulfed the whole airplane. We watched in horror, unable to do anything but yell, "Bail out, you guys. Bail out!" As it continued to roll to an inverted position, a grinding explosion ripped the air. Men and metal were scattered across the sky. For long moments, our eyes followed smoldering bits falling earthward. That was all that could be seen of a very large airplane and ten men.

Returning our attention to the bomb run, we discovered that the Me-110 slowed to allow us to fly under him. Panic gushed through us as the death rain began. Bullets came smashing down through the wings and fuselage. In the distance, we could see the fighters grouping for their three-pronged attack. I knew we might not survive the next few minutes.

Pushing the intercom button, I said to my top gunner, "Gunderson, get both barrels ready. I'm going to pull right up into his gut. You'll only get one shot."

Gunderson didn't get a chance to answer. Almost immediately, Colonel Austin ordered, "Stay on target, Hawkins."

I disengaged the autopilot and said to my bombardier, "I've got it, Herb."

The intercom reverberated as Colonel Austin shouted, "Captain Hawkins, stay on the bomb run."

I answered with full power and a forceful pull on the control wheel. The 50,000-pound Fortress groaned as it zoomed upward. Colonel Austin shouted in disbelief, "Hawkins, you've broken formation!" But we now stood barrel to barrel with the surprised Messerschmitt.

At point-blank range, we invited a duel. I knew Bob Gunderson was good. He was well trained and had proven himself under fire. His two guns blazed against the German's four, but he knew right where to place his stream of fifty-caliber bullets. Within seconds, the Me-110 burst into flames and wheeled into a spin. No one got out of the stricken Messerschmitt.

The intercom was flooded with cheers from the crew. As the noise subsided, Colonel Austin growled, "Hawkins, get this airplane back into formation and on the bomb run."

"Yes, sir," I answered.

"And remember, you're no hot-rock fighter pilot; you're a bomber pilot."

"Yes sir," I acknowledged while reengaging the autopilot.

"You've got it, Herb."

Colonel Austin and I knew that we could not reestablish the required ground track for a precision bomb run, but for now, the Colonel seemed willing to forgive my transgression because we were alive.

Shooting down the Me-110 might have been a mistake. The thirty-odd fighters directed by the downed aircraft decided to make us pay for the death of their friends. They disregarded all the other bombers and concentrated on us. Although their attack now lacked the previous coordination, it was vastly fiercer. They barreled in from all six sides, lashing our Fortress with machine-gun and cannon fire. The gunners fought back, but the Germans were overwhelming. The tide of battle quickly turned their way. As we moved closer to the target, flak bursts began to fill the sky around us. The sharp, jagged pieces of steel that came screaming out of those ugly black puffs ripped and clawed at soft aluminum and flesh alike.

As hideous as it was, the flak had one grace: the fighters would back off for fear of being hit by their own flak shells—or so we thought. To our surprise, the German fighter pilots, in their determination to destroy us, dared their own flak and continued to press the attack. It became obvious that we would be killed.

A piece of shrapnel from an exploding flak shell smashed into Ron Bailey's leg. In addition to a three-inch gash in his leg, his lower leg bone was broken. Colonel Austin applied a compression binding to stop the bleeding, but the steel fragment remained embedded in the leg. Nothing could be done for the broken bone. Bailey stayed seated at his radio station. Operating his gun was impossible. Colonel Austin took over the radio operator's gun and joined the fight, only to be hit. A single machine-gun slug passed through his right hand and lodged in his left bicep. Colonel Austin fell away from the gun, unable to use either hand. Although seriously injured, both were alive.

Bob Mason was the first to die. He went quickly with a 20mm cannon shell that ripped away a good portion of the fuselage skin near Bill Jackson's feet. The top half of Danny's auburn-haired beauty went with it. The frigid air blasting through the gaping hole was less chilling than the loss of our navigator.

The fighter attacks grew more intense and the flak thickened. I was anxious and asked the bombardier, "How much longer, Herb?"

"About 10 miles to bomb release."

"Can we last?" I asked myself. As if to answer the question, a violent explosion, heard over the roaring engines and raging machine guns, jerked the Fortress into a dangerous yaw. As the autopilot canceled the yaw, she wallowed into a left bank and hung there, wing low. Listing like a stricken ship at sea, we struggled to stay aloft. The airspeed dwindled. I knew we had taken a bad hit and expected "Danny's Dream" to begin breaking up.

I jerked at the mike to order preparations for a bailout when someone tripped the intercom switch ahead of me and our headsets were filled with screaming. It was a scream of great pain. It was a scream with the power of a man, but the tearful shrillness of an injured child. It was Tubbs. He cried, "I'm hit! I'm hit!"

I answered, "Tubbs, can you give me a damage report?"

The answer came, "Help me, Captain. Help me." My headset remained full of agonized, tearful crying.

It only took me an instant to make up my mind. We couldn't afford to have another gunner away from his guns, and I had confidence in Bill Jackson's ability to fly the airplane. I would go help Tubbs and see how badly our Fortress had been hit. I pressed the intercom button and ordered, "Gunners, stay at your stations. I'll help Tubbs."

I flashed a "You've got it" sign toward my copilot. Giving me a thumbs-up sign, Bill grasped the controls with a smile. I hooked up to a portable oxygen bottle and started back to the gunners' compartment.

The explosion we heard was a flak shell or a rocket right up the gut. The blast had torn away a section of the fuselage between the bomb bay and the gunners. The hole looked large enough to drive a jeep through. Twisted pieces of steel and aluminum littered the compartment. Much of the ship's insulating material and some of the gunners' clothing were smoking and smoldering. The lack of oxygen at our altitude and the violent wind whistling through the cabin prevented fire. Surveying the damage, I was amazed that the fuselage had not buckled and broken.

Looking beyond the damaged area, I could see that I had ordered dead men to continue manning their guns. Al Martin dangled across his left waist gun with two perfectly round holes about an inch apart in his forehead. The ball turret had taken the main blast and pieces of Shorty Rogers remained.

Tubbs was screaming and rolling on the floor, clawing at his right leg and crying. His right boot and one lucky sock were blown completely off. His bare foot was a mass of mangled flesh and shattered bone. Hanging loosely at the ankle, it was attached to his leg by only an inch of flesh. Blood was pumping out in ugly spurts and freezing solid as it splashed on the aluminum walkway.

Tubbs cried, "Cut it off, Captain. Please," thinking that if the foot was gone it would no longer hurt.

"Tubbs, we've got to get a tourniquet on to stop the bleeding."
I ripped open his pant leg, fashioned a tourniquet from a mike cord,
and twisted it hard. The bleeding stopped, but he continued to
cry with the pain. Each time he tossed, the foot flopped from side
to side. I took a morphine capsule from the medical kit and said,
"You're going to be all right, Tubbs. This will make you feel better."
I rammed the needle deep into his leg and squeezed in the fluid.
The morphine would dull his brain and let him forget most of his
pain.

Something had to be done with the foot. Perhaps it could be
saved. I squeezed the mass of flesh together, positioned it at the
end of his leg, and began taping it in place. I wound yards of
adhesive tape around the foot and ankle. It looked more like a big
ball than a foot.

While I was working on Tubbs, the fighter and antiaircraft
barrage continued. Between flak bursts I could hear the tail guns
bucking. Using Tubbs' headset and mike, I called, "Manning, you
all right back there?"

"I ain't dead yet, Captain, but I'm almost out of ammo."

"Well, if you run out, just keep wagging those guns around
so they'll know you ain't dead, and they'll keep their distance."

"Yes sir," came his reply. He gave me no indication that he
had been shot and was trying to dress his wounds between fighter
assaults.

Tubbs reached up and clutched my arm. "How's Al and Shorty
doing, Captain?"

There's no easy way to say it so I just said it. "They're dead,
Tubby." I could tell the news hurt him as much as his foot.

Knowing that the tail guns were now our only defense, Tubbs
said, "We ain't doing too good, are we, Captain?"

"We're doing just fine. Herb should be dropping his bombs
soon and then we'll be headed home."

"I mean we ain't got no defense against those fighters now,
do we?"

A spray of machine-gun bullets ripped through the
compartment, scattering bits of aluminum skin to emphasize his
point. "Will you help me back to my gun?"

He was pale from the loss of blood. He could easily die of shock.
I answered, "No, Tubbs. You've done enough for today. You just
stay down and rest easy. I'll fly us home."

I felt like I was lying to him because I knew our Fortress couldn't take much more. I left the sergeant lying on the floor shivering in the bitter cold and started working my way forward again.

I was greeted by a horror. The entire forward section had been blasted by flak and machine-gun fire. The Plexiglas nose was blown away by flak. The bombsight stood erect in the gaping hole, glaring at Germany through open space and freezing air, but the bombardier was not there to share in its defiance. Herb Tollison had been blown to the rear of the compartment. He died instantly. We were still carrying the bombs.

Bob Gunderson hung lifeless in the top turret. A row of machine-gun bullet holes dimpled the back of his flight jacket.

One of the German machine-gun slugs from the volley that had killed Gunderson had ricocheted off the breech of his Browning and struck Bill Jackson in the neck. Blood was bubbling up around his collar and running down his front, but he was alive. A tourniquet was impossible. I grabbed a compress from the medical kit and forced it under his collar and pressed down hard. The bleeding slowed, but within seconds he gagged and blood ran from his mouth. The slug went completely through to his throat. Stopping the bleeding on the outside only forced it inside. He was going to bleed to death or drown in his own blood.

Bill Jackson knew nothing could save him. He clutched my hands working frantically at his neck and said, "Jettison the bomb load, Captain."

I slumped into my seat. A feeling of total desperation overcame me because of my inability to help him. I slammed my fist into the control column again and again. Punishing the airplane and inflicting pain on myself was the only possible response.

I thought of the bombs again and toggled them away with a vengeance. I didn't care what they hit. I wished they could kill every man, woman, and child in Germany.

Bill sensed my frustration. He reached across the narrow space between us and gripped my clenched fist. He looked at me and tried to smile over the pain of his injury and the knowledge that he was dying. It was a weak smile, but it showed the real courage in the man. His eyes flickered and dimmed as death was near. He leaned closer and removed his oxygen mask to speak without the interphone. I quickly put my ear close to his mouth because the words would be weak.

"You believe me now, don't you?" I turned my face briefly toward him as if to ask, "What are you talking about?" and returned my ear to his mouth.

He whispered, "The Virgin Mary, she's got you in her arms. Look around you, Captain. Everybody's dead or bleeding, and you don't have a scratch."

Overwhelmed by massive feelings of guilt, I said, "Bill, I shouldn't have left you alone."

He struggled to answer as his life dripped slowly to the cabin floor. "The Holy Mother loves you."

His eyes closed and he fell limp. I thought he was gone. His body jerked. He gasped and his voice gurgled through the blood in his throat. Through the mumbled words I heard,"...use it..."

With that, Bill Jackson slipped away. And with that the fighting stopped. Magdeburg was behind us. The enemy retreated to survey the damage and count its dead. We had lost 85 airplanes; 970 men were killed and 1,020 were injured. All that remained was getting "Danny's Dream" on the ground and it would be over.

Tubby Tubbs got the Medal of Honor. When a Medal of Honor is awarded, the words that go along with it include phrase like "conspicuous bravery," "concern for comrades," "disregard for personal safety," "utmost desire to complete the mission," and "action above and beyond the call of duty." All of these describe what Tubbs did at Magdeburg. Overcoming the pain of his critical injury, the loss of a great deal of blood, and the mind-fogging drugs I gave him, and working alone, he struggled back to his waist gun on his taped-up foot.

Fighting like an inspired madman, he leaped from the right waist gun to the left and back and forth as the battle shifted from side to side. Resisting the extreme cold and high winds whipping through the blast-torn aft fuselage, he managed to connect his electrically heated suit and oxygen mask only when time permitted. He fought for long periods without them, exposing himself to extreme environmental conditions. Suffering frostbite to his foot, fingers, and face, he stood off three squadrons of German fighters, destroying six and damaging many more.

He sustained additional serious injuries from enemy machine-gun fire to his left arm and leg, but he continued to man his guns. Reloading the waist guns with ammunition from the damaged ball turret, he continued firing to the battle's end.

He was credited with saving the ship with command responsibility, the mission commander, and the ship's crew. He thus contributed significantly to the successful completion of the mission. But the foot was lost; he was going home.

Bill Jackson, copilot; Herb Tollison, bombardier; Bob Mason, navigator; Bob Gunderson, top gunner; Al Martin, left waist gunner; and Shorty Rogers, ball turret gunner—all had flown their last mission. They would never go home. We four survivors saluted when our six friends and crewmates were lowered into the ground. Colonel Austin, in an unusual gesture, sent the corporal from headquarters to play taps. He was occasionally off key, but we didn't mind. It added a certain military dignity to the otherwise simple burial given by the Army, and it was our last farewell to some very good men.

When it was over, I turned to look at the others. Manning and Bailey, struggling with their casts and crutches, were returning to the truck that had brought them to this remote spot of English soil. The nurse sent to push Tubbs along in his wheelchair stood like a sentinel behind him; she seemed protective. Although she was a captain, she was obviously proud to care for a sergeant who had won the Medal of Honor.

Tubbs sat quietly in the wheelchair staring at the graves. Tears streaked his round cheeks. I stepped between him and the graves to face him squarely. "Well, Tubbs, you're going home this afternoon. I guess this is goodbye."

"Yes, sir, but I sure hate to leave you..." he paused, looked through me at the six graves and added,"...and the rest of our guys. We were a great crew, weren't we, Captain?"

"Yeah, Tubbs, the best. I'm sorry it has to end like this."

Cheerfulness arose in this strong man. He managed a smile and said, "It really hasn't ended for me, Captain. I'm going to look up our guys' families when I get home. You know, Shorty and me, we were good buddies. I'm going to see his folks and tell them what a brave man he was and that he didn't suffer."

"And Lieutenant Tollison, well, sometimes he'd have trouble writing his girl. He always had good thoughts. He just couldn't get them down on paper. I'd read her letters and help him with his answers. I got to know her real good. She's like a sister to me. I'll go see her after I get my new foot and learn how to walk again."

The longer he talked, the happier he became. I could see that he was putting his loss behind him and looking ahead.

"That's great, Tubby. I can see that you're going to be all right."

"And you're going to be all right too, Captain. You've just got one more to go and you'll be on your way home too."

Not wanting to reveal a decision that I had made earlier that day, I answered with a reassuring smile, "That's right, Tubby. I've got it made, so don't worry about me. You just take care of yourself."

Tubbs fumbled in his pocket and withdrew one ordinary, standard issue, olive drab U.S. Army sock. "Captain, I want you to have my lucky sock. I'm sorry there's only one, but..." His words trailed off as his eyes fell to his missing foot. Looking back, he continued, "Take it with you. It'll get you through"

"Aw, Tubbs, I couldn't take your sock. You'll want to keep it."

Pushing the sock into my hand, he said, "No, I want you to have it, Captain. Please."

The nurse interrupted. "Take the sock, Captain. I've got to get Sergeant Tubbs back to the base to catch his airplane. He's going to the White House, you know."

Taking the sock, I said, "So long, Tubbs. You're a great guy." I came to attention and saluted the sergeant.

Tubbs' round face flushed red and he said, "Aw, Captain. You don't have to salute me."

While holding my salute, I said, "Tubbs, every man of every rank of every branch of the service will be required to salute you because you're going to get the Medal of Honor. I'm saluting you because you are the bravest man I have ever known." He turned a little redder, smiled a proud smile, and returned my salute.

I patted him on the shoulder, winked a final goodbye, and said, "Thanks for the lucky sock." Tubbs smiled in return as the nurse wheeled him toward the truck.

I turned back to face the military cemetery and the sea of white crosses that grew after each mission. I could feel the presence of all the brave young men silently resting there in neat rows. The six open graves where my crewmen lay stood in contrast. Their graves would be filled, and the crosses at my feet would be placed after we departed.

Kneeling, I fumbled through the stack of crosses until coming to the one labeled JACKSON, WILLIAM R., 1ST LT. Picking it up, I said, "Bill, I sure hope you're right about the Virgin Mary. I'm going to need her protection a whole lot. You told me to use it, so I am. I'm going to stay and continue flying."

Bill Jackson and Tubbs removed my fear of the last mission jinx. If there was truth in Bill's belief and some of Tubb's courage hidden in his sock, I could stay and put to good use the protection and courage they left me. For me, there would be no last mission until the war was over.

SOBERING
UP

IT WAS TUESDAY, NOVEMBER 28, 1933. A COLD FRONT had passed during the night, leaving a clear blue sky and a chilly north wind. The overnight temperature had dropped to near freezing. Although it was midmorning and the sun sparkled in the crystalline sky, it remained cold. Mother insisted that I wear a heavy leather jacket over several layers of clothing. I put on my helmet and goggles, and Bo tied a scarf around my face and neck in western bandit style. He also insisted that I wear his heavy gloves. As we stood before the biplane, there wasn't one square inch of my skin exposed. I looked ready for an assault on the North Pole.

Following a careful preflight inspection, Bo said, "O.k., boy, here's what we're gonna do. I'm just gonna ride in the front cockpit while you take it around and shoot a few landings. That'll get you and the airplane warmed up. Then, if everything is working right, I'm getting out and it's all yours." I nodded my understanding, not daring to use words for fear that a nervous tremble might be detected in my voice. I was tense.

Mothers have a way of knowing things about their sons and mine asked, ''Are you sure about this, Mr. Wages?''

''Yes, ma'am. He's the best I've ever seen. He's a regular Charles Lindbergh.''

Hearing Bo's words of confidence helped immensely. Warmth oozed through my body and some of the tension eased. Being belted into the rear cockpit and hearing the Ford's friendly ''clapity plap clapity plap'' helped even more. As we taxied toward the take-off point, I began to feel a little more at home and ready for my first solo flight.

With Bo's head nodding approval from the front cockpit, I slowly opened the throttle wide and began a careful take-off run. The cool morning air quickly buoyed the airplane aloft. Having the take-off go so well strengthened my confidence. Relaxing further, I circled our pasture landing strip and wagged my wings at the small figure standing at its edge. Mother waved both arms in a return greeting. After several steep turns and a playful zoom climb, Bo had had enough of my ''warming up'' exercises and signaled me to return for the landings.

On the first attempt at landing, I forced myself to imagine that Bo was not in the front cockpit. I tried to visualize being solo. Imagining that he was not there to help me and that the successful outcome of the landing was entirely up to me, I tried very hard. I aligned the airplane directly into the wind, kept the wings absolutely level, carefully controlled attitude and airspeed, used the power to control sink rate and approach path, smoothly flared as the ground approached, and made a near perfect landing without the least bounce.

My reward came quickly. Bo raised his right hand with thumb and forefinger touching, signaling o.k.

My confidence surged toward cockiness. I roughly gunned the Ford to full power for another take-off. Bo sensed my cockiness and half looked back over his shoulder, but had nothing to say or signal. Circling the field again, there was no doubt in my mind. I knew that I could fly and land the biplane. I easily convinced myself that I was the master of the machine and of the air. My ego told me that I was a great pilot. I could do anything and everything in the air. I could only think of myself and how good I was.

Being drunk on the alcohol of egotism resulted in a lack of attention. I neglected the details of airspeed, altitude, power setting, and sink rate. As the point of landing neared, I suddenly realized that I was too high and too slow, and had developed a high sink rate. As I uttered a gasp, my mind commanded: "power."

Jamming the throttle open too fast and too much caused the Ford to belch and stumble. The flight situation deteriorated further as the biplane wallowed near a stall and sank rapidly toward a crash.

The Ford finally recovered from the burst I had tried to force upon it and roared to life. The sudden surge of excess power caused the biplane to roll and yaw left. The nose came up and all forward vision disappeared. I suddenly had a handful of airplane that was ahead of its pilot and on the edge of a disaster.

Trying to regain control of the airplane, I jammed the stick and rudder right, while reducing power and lowering the nose. Again, I had done too much too late and too fast. I wasn't thinking; I was reacting. The airplane half rolled, half fell, and half skidded into the ground. The right main landing gear dug deeply into the grass and everything became a circular blur as the biplane pirouetted through a ground loop.

We had gone through one-and-a-half turns before coming to rest and were facing opposite the landing direction. The Ford was putt-putting at a smooth idle, but there was a morguelike silence.

Slowly Bo raised and turned in the front cockpit to face me. His face was red and swollen as his anger tried to burst from behind his tightly pinched lips. Then, after a deep breath that flared his nostrils, he said through clenched teeth, "That is the most stupid thing I have ever seen you do! I don't care if you wreck this airplane. I don't even care if you kill yourself, but I'll be darned if I'll let you embarrass me in front of your ma. I told her you was good and, by duggers, you're gonna be good or else. The difference in those two landings you just did was not the airplane, and not the wind. The whole difference was in your head. Flying is a thinking man's activity. It's not for boys. Now, either you get the right attitude about this flying or you get out and go back to milking cows."

I was devastated. Three explosive depressions had occurred within me. The first blow was having failed to control the airplane and being helplessly charioted through a ground loop. I had never done such a poor job before, nor have I since. The second blow was the enormous embarrassment of having my only flying mishap witnessed by my mother. And the last blow was Bo's ultimatum.

I couldn't respond. I was numb. My mind reverberated with the shock waves.

Huffily, Bo faced forward in his cockpit and, in cavalry fashion, gruffly signaled me ahead once more. Extremely sober now, I thought out every motion and used smooth, measured control inputs while circling and landing. Getting thoughts of myself out of my mind and concentrating fully on the operation of the airplane and on fundamental flying techniques, I completed three near-perfect take-offs and landings. On the third landing roll-out, Bo signaled me to stop. I knew that my time to solo had come and a slight uneasiness gripped my stomach.

Bo rolled out of the front cockpit and stood facing me squarely. Standing on the wing, he towered over me like a giant. He stood there and looked squarely into my eyes with a firmly set jaw. I was expecting a stern lecture on the demands of solo flight when suddenly a giant smile broke across his face that stretched his mustache from ear to ear. Giving me a small boxer's punch on the chin and a wink he said, "You're gonna like this, boy. Go fly around the dairy barn so's your Pa can see you, and then come back and shoot three good landings, and don't go getting cocky on me. Keep your mind on good flying."

With that, he bounded off the wing and joined my mother as a spectator. I was alone and very sober.

 # SOLO

D URING MY "WARM UP" FLIGHT WITH BO, I DIS-
covered that it was possible for a person to be very cold
and sweat at the same time. The chill factor in the open
cockpit was below zero. I still shivered, but as I shivered, a trickle
of sweat worked its way down my spine, and my palms were moist.
I maneuvered the biplane to the far end of the field, turned to the
take-off direction, and sat motionless. The wind whispered through
the wires urging me to join it aloft.

I studied the biplane. It seemed bigger and boxier than before,
but somehow lighter as it answered the wind with a gentle rocking
from side to side. I stretched right to see around the forward fuselage and radiator. Through the arc of the slowly turning propeller, I could see the full length of the pasture ahead of me. Stretching
to the left, I saw two figures with their backs turned against the
cold north wind awaiting my take-off. My mother was clasped
tightly in her own arms trying to ward off the November chill. Bo
had his hands thrust deeply into his pockets. I looked down and
saw his gloves on my hands and felt his strength and conviction.

The Ford belched a little puff of black smoke from its exhaust, drawing my attention back to the task at hand. It was time for me to solo, to fly alone. I eased the throttle open.

While practicing take-offs, Bo had repeatedly told me, "You use all of your senses on the take-off, boy. If it don't look right, feel right, sound right, or smell right, shut it down and stop."

I recalled this teaching as clearly as if Bo were there whispering in my ear. All my senses were needle sharp and reached out for any warning that all might not be well. But all *was* well and the biplane screamed into the air as I flashed by my two huddled spectators.

The biplane's vigor amazed me. The speed jumped to ninety and the altimeter was spinning as never before. "The climb speed should be seventy," I muttered and raised the nose to get a steeper climb and slower speed. The altitude increased even more rapidly. My plan was to level at 1,000 feet above our pasture, but by the time the speed settled on seventy, the biplane had zoomed to 1,500 feet. I worked hard to get the nose down and the power back to a cruise setting; I felt droplets of sweat building on my forehead. The open cockpit wind-blast bit through my clothing, and I shivered a brief chill under my sweat. Finally, I got the biplane set up for level cruise at 1,700 feet. The dairy barn was below and slightly to my left.

Descending slightly and circling to my left, I zoomed around the barn at an altitude that I thought my father would think safe. On my second pass around the barn, father came out, shielding his eyes against the morning sun. Still circling left, I saw him wave at me. I waggled my wings in return. Then, on closer look, I saw a milk bucket in his left hand. Perhaps he wasn't waving but was signaling me to return to work. I broke out of my barn-circling turn and headed for the pasture landing field.

Until now, my full attention had been focused on the demands of the flight. I had given no thought to being solo. Heading for the pasture, however, the airplane was trimmed well and comfortably easing its way through smooth air. My attention fell on the gaping hole in front of me. It seemed strange not seeing Bo sitting there waving his hands or shouting at me. Although I knew that I was alone from the moment Bo got out of the airplane, the full realization didn't hit until I began to study the empty front cockpit.

It caused a strange confusion of feelings to arise within me. I was happy to be solo. I was even proud to be solo. But I was surprised to realize that I didn't feel a great thrill from being solo. While rebuilding the biplane and taking lessons leading to my solo flight, I had convinced myself that the first solo flight would be an enthralling experience. I expected my insides to reverberate with escalating waves of excitement. Instead, I found myself evaluating my own airmanship. "Your recovery from climb to cruise was terrible because you missed your altitude by 700 feet!" I was confused by the conflict between expectation and realization, and wondered if something was wrong with me for not being thrilled. Approaching the landing field, my attention returned to the next big event: my first solo landing.

Recalling my disastrous approach to landing and the resulting embarrassment an hour earlier, I concentrated fully on flying the airplane with good fundamental techniques. While Bo and mother watched carefully, I eased the biplane toward the final approach. Much less stick force was required to flare to a landing without Bo in the front cockpit. I slightly overcontrolled and the biplane ballooned away from the runway. Careful not to repeat my mistakes of earlier that morning, I applied small, smooth control corrections. I was rewarded when all three wheels touched the grass in a near-perfect landing. Adding power, I made the second take-off, circled, and landed again. Repeating the take-off and landing a third time, my first solo flight was completed as laid out by Bo. I taxied the airplane toward the tiedown.

Amid Bo's handshaking and backslapping, and mother's hugs, I felt great pride in the accomplishment, but dared not mention the confused feelings that still wrestled within me. As time passed, I tried many times to relive my first solo flight. I tried to generate the excitement that I had expected but somehow missed on that one day in my life; I always failed.

More than a year after my solo, I finally confessed to Bo my failure to be excited on the first solo. When I heard his words, I wished that I had told him on that cold November morning a year earlier. Bo said simply, "That's fine, boy. You shouldn't be excited by it. That tells me you're no joy-rider. That tells me you're an aviator. You see, there's excitement and satisfaction. Aviators get satisfaction from good airmanship. Leave excitement to the thrill seekers."

AIR, WIND, AND WEATHER

I HAD SOLOED BO'S BIPLANE A WEEK EARLIER. BO WAS proud of me and bragged at length about my flight. He often concluded with, "Why, that boy could teach Wilbur and Orville a thing or two."

At first, I took his words in stride, but as he continued to brag about me and my flying, I began to believe his lavish praise. Little by little, exaggerated self-confidence grew within me. I think Bo sensed my overconfidence and looked for a way to ease my self-esteem back to earth.

We were working on a barn door that had been blown off its hinges the day before. It was hard work and the day was unusually warm for early December. As the sun reached its zenith, we were perspiring freely as we worked. Bo stepped back from the work, wiped his brow, and said, "That's Texas for you. One day it blows the doors off the hinges and the next it's so still you can barely pull in enough air to stay alive. This air requires a lot of study."

"Why do you say that, Bo?"

"Well, if you're going to fly airplanes, you have to know about the air."

Feeling cocky after having Bo brag so much about my flying, I said, "What's there to know about the air? Air is air!"

"Not so fast, boy. There's more to it than you think. I'd bet you don't even know what wind is. Tell me, what is wind?"

"Wind? That's like asking me about the air. Air is air and wind is wind. The wind just blows."

"You see. You don't know, do you?"

"Well...." When I thought about it, I admitted that he was right. I didn't know.

Bo instructed, "The wind is nothing more than air in motion. When there ain't no wind, we say it's calm, but we still have the air to breathe and fly in. It's when the air starts to move that we have wind."

"Yeah, I can see that," I responded.

"Good, but there's even more to it than that"

"Oh?" He had my interest now.

"Yes, there is. The air can have four different motions, and only one of them is called *wind*."

"Now, look, Bo, you ain't trying to—?"

"No, boy. This is 'meterlology.' The air really can move in four different ways. You see, the air can move roughly parallel to the earth's surface. That's the motion of the air that we call *wind*. But the air can also move vertically upward. When it does that, we call it an *updraft*. A couple of special updrafts here in Texas are thermals and thunderstorm convection. Also, the air can move vertically downward. When it does that, we call it a *downdraft*.

"Downdrafts are mostly the result of updrafts. You can see that if the air in an updraft just kept moving up, soon there wouldn't be any air left at the bottom of the updraft. The downdraft gets the air back down to the bottom. So, for every updraft, there's got to be a downdraft somewhere. And these up- and downdrafts are the things that we feel as 'bumps' when we fly."

"The last motion of the air can be the most dangerous, and that's when it twists around itself. In this motion, the air is swirling around in a tight circle. When it moves like that, we call it a *twister*. The kinds of twisters that we see here in Texas are dust devils and tornados. You see that, boy?"

By now I realized that Bo was teaching a serious lesson, and I respectfully answered, "Yes, sir."

"O.k. You see that the air can have four different motions. Now let's get down to the air itself. The air we got here in Texas is kind of special, kind of wild, and always hard to understand."

"You mean our air ain't like everybody else's?"

"Not by a long shot! For one thing, the air here is made up of Gulf air, and Mexican air, and Pacific air, and North Pole air. And then each one of them airs can be hot air, or cold air, or wet air, or dry air. They can combine to become sixteen different kinds of air. Sometimes these different airs get along pretty good and swirl all around together. Sometimes they back off into separate piles and battle for the right to sit on a certain piece of Texas."

"What do you mean, 'battle'?" I questioned.

"I mean like war, boy, where things get destroyed and people get hurt."

"Like war?"

"Sure thing. Sometimes it's a big, full-blown, all-out war, and sometimes it's just a little shoot-out. It all depends on how different the kinds of air are from each other and how fast they charge into one another."

"One of the worst wars happens when a big blob of warm, wet air comes floating in off the Gulf and stakes its claim to a million miles of Texas. Just then a tremendous pile of cold, dry air that is sitting up in the panhandle decides it wants the same piece of land. So it starts to move south. Now there's air in motion, or wind. You can always tell when that cold blob of air goes by where you're standing because the temperature drops and the wind shifts around from the north or northwest. Anyway, it comes roaring down across the state and those two big blobs collide along a thousand-mile battle front. That's when the fireworks start."

Bo knew by my wide-eyed stare that he had hold of my mind and continued, "The first thing that happens is that all along the front, the clouds shoot up higher than any man has ever been in an airplane. And they get big enough around to cover whole counties. Just one of those clouds would make Mount Everest look like a molehill. They sit there and churn and boil and then after a while they get real mean. There are very few things that can hold together inside one of those boiling, swirling monsters. That's sure no place to be in an airplane. Then, as the battle develops, they shoot out crackling hot bolts of lightning that splits trees, kills cows, and sets fire to barns and fields. Often as not they put out their own fires by dumping rain by the buckets all along the front."

"You know, just one inch of rain on a section of land amounts to about 18 million gallons of water. Some of these frog stranglers we had around here before the drought would cover four or five sections and dump four or five inches of rain in an hour. That's about 400 million gallons of water in an hour and the cause of some of our flash flooding. When rains like that hit, an otherwise dry little creek bed may have a wall of water six to ten feet high roaring down it."

I was breathless. I gasped for some air and realized that he was talking about the innocent little stuff that I had just breathed in.

He saw that I was impressed and added, "But the worst is sometimes yet to come. Sometimes, as the war reaches its peak, those clouds dump tons and tons of hail on people and things. I've seen it hail so hard that cows were killed, crops destroyed, and the roofs beat off barns and houses."

Speaking slowly now with stiffened lips and squinted eyelids, he said, "And then, every once in a while, an especially mean cloud will let the dark snaky tail of a tornado dip down to rip and claw at the land. And so the battle goes on, doing lots of damage and hurting folks that get in the way."

Eager to participate in the exciting images he drew in my mind, I chirped, "We've had some hailstorms go through here, Bo."

"Sure you have, boy. And did you notice that they moved along after a while?"

"Yes. I did."

"Well, you see, most of the time one kind of air will win the battle and push the other air back where it came from. So the battle front moves along. But sometimes both sides run out of ammunition; they just stall out, call a truce, and gradually mix and mingle together."

I was tremendously moved. I not only gained a new and startling view of the air around me, but could see that I knew very little about this business of flying. The arrogant self-confidence that had started building within me suddenly died. I was wondering what other simple things like the air would come to amaze me.

Bo could see that I was speechless and said, "You can see from all this how important it is for us to know where the different kinds of air are located and which way they are likely to move." I nodded again.

"Because we sure don't want to get caught right in the big middle of one of them battles," he admonished.

"Noooo, sir," I agreed.

"Well, we've only talked about one small piece of this business. Different kinds of air running together act in different ways. There's a lot more to be learned and understood than what we've just talked about. When we go to Houston on your cross-country flight, I'm going to take you to the Weather Bureau. That's where they keep track of all these different kinds of air and which way they're moving. You'll be able to see a weather map that shows the whole thing in one look."

I couldn't believe that some people understood all this and could draw maps of it. As I wondered at it all, a question arose in my mind. "But if these battle fronts are always moving around, how can they put them on a map?"

"They draw a new map every three hours. And they do some other things to keep up with all the weather that affects our flying. You'll like meeting those folks."

"I sure will, Bo."

"And if you're lucky, they might have a book on 'meterlology' that you can buy. So be sure to take some money along."

Our trip to Houston was no longer just a cross-country training flight; it assumed a greater importance. I eagerly looked forward to meeting the men at the Weather Bureau and getting into the study of meteorology. I was learning again.

A
MEDAL
FOR
OLD
SOGGY

A FTER D-DAY, MOST OF THE U.S. ARMY'S LOGISTIC effort was spent in supporting the Allied armies as they advanced across France. The Germans fought fiercely and yielded French soil only foot by bloody foot. The great need was for the men and materials for the land war. For much too long, logistic support for the air war was limited to bombs, bullets, and fuel. The airplanes and crews became increasingly tattered as replacements were not to be found.

No matter how severely a B-17 was shredded by enemy fire, the ground crews could always find enough scrap metal to patch it up again, but the engines were another story. New or freshly overhauled engines were as rare as a Christmas package from home. Only two ways existed to get a fresh engine installed in an airplane: either an engine had to be demolished, or it had to be completely worn out. The big question was, "When is an engine completely worn out?" Colonel Austin, the group commander, answered with

134

his personal standard, "An engine is worn out when it burns all of its oil!"

The B-17 had four 15-gallon oil tanks, one for each engine. Before each mission they were filled to capacity. Upon returning from the mission, they were carefully checked. If any tank had oil remaining at mission end, the tank was refilled and that engine stayed in service. If the tank was empty, the engine was changed.

With that criteria for an engine change, it didn't take an overly bright crew to figure out how to get a fresh engine. Each pilot tried to destroy his poorest engine by operational abuse. While keeping three engines well within normal operating ranges, the weak engine could be safely pressed to destruction by exceeding all operating limits. And this is exactly what we planned to do with Old Soggy.

Old Soggy was the number three engine on our Fortress. It had been sitting there on the right wing, grinding away since the airplane left the factory and it had outlived three crews before us. In terms of operating hours, it had gone nearly twice the manufactuer's recommended overhaul time. Every other part on the airplane had been replaced or repaired, but not Old Soggy. Orange and blue flames hissed from its leaky exhaust system. It always smelled of leaking fuel and dripped oil from every seal and gasket. Many of its cooling fins had been chipped away by enemy fire.

It missed and sputtered at low speed and ran with a surging lope at high speed. Always soggy and wet with seeping oil and grime, Old Soggy was both the ugliest and most miserable-looking piece of machinery I had ever seen, but it always came home with about a gallon of oil in its oil tank. The crew and I felt that Old Soggy would let us down at some critical moment when we needed a good engine. We decided that something had to be done.

The upcoming mission was supposed to be a milk run, so we would have no fighter escort. Most of our fighters were committed to a simultaneous attack on a heavily defended target by other bombers. The mission planners conceded that a few of our aircraft "might suffer some light damage" and grudgingly assigned one squadron of fighters to meet us on the way home. Most of our missions were anything but milk runs, so we decided that we might never have a better opportunity. I told our ground crew to get a fresh engine ready. This time out we were going to put the screws to Old Soggy. We would either blow it up or burn it up. Our plan was to wait until we bombed the target and departed the drop zone.

Then, if there were no enemy resistance, we would put the rpm, the manifold pressure, the mixture, the cylinder head temperature, the oil temperature, everything, at or beyond red-line limits and hold them there until Old Soggy gave up the ghost.

We dropped our bombs on the lightly guarded target and headed back toward England. We encountered no fighters and we had no flak damage. It looked like a milk run in the making. The time was right. I eased numbers one, two, and four back a little for safety and jammed Old Soggy's propeller control to its limit. Old Soggy howled up to the rpm red line. Shoving the manifold pressure up to the maximum caused Old Soggy to begin its uneven high-speed surge. Setting the mixture to its leanest and hottest setting caused intense blue flames to spew out everywhere. With the cowl flaps closed, the cylinder head temperature leaped toward its limit. Closing the oil cooler shutters caused the oil temperature to surge past its red line. "What a brutal thing to do," I thought, then quickly reasoned, "But they shoot crippled horses."

The Wright Cyclone engine in our Fortress was limited to three minutes operating at maximum power. Our plan was to hold Old Soggy beyond the limit for more than three hours if necessary. I stretched my neck a little to sneak a look past my copilot. Old Soggy was out there pounding and clamoring as hard as it could. Its life-blood was trickling out over the cowling and wing. Some of the oil bubbled and played in the slipstream. Some of it fried in the blistering blue flames of the exhaust. Much of it trailed behind, drawing a dark line through those hostile German skies. I felt ashamed of what we were doing and imagined that Old Soggy, without missing one strained beat, looked back to ask, "Why? Why this?" I looked away in guilt and tried to convince myself that we were doing the right thing for our ship and our own safety.

There is something eerie about seeing all the engine parameters at or beyond red line, especially when it is done on purpose. Even before I learned to fly, I had been taught to take care of my machinery. It was hard to put down my feelings of wrong doing. While focusing inwardly on these feelings of guilt, a blinding flash and piercing explosion to my left jerked me back to reality. The glass of my pilot's side window was shattered. Through it I saw smoke, flame, and sparks flashing from the number two engine as it thrashed itself to bits. Quickly activating the propeller feathering control had no effect; there was no longer a propeller out there. It departed the airplane with the front half of the engine and most of the cowling. There was only an ugly stub where number two had been.

I thought the number two engine had a sudden mechanical failure, but then another Fortress in the formation burst into flames. We had been jumped by enemy fighters. Coming undetected out of the sun, they surprised us and inflicted a great deal of damage on several airplanes. Our number two engine hadn't failed; it had taken a 20mm cannon shell squarely in the crankcase. Our milk run was turning into a nightmare as the intercom was alive with reports of enemy fighters everywhere.

As the fight developed, I quickly got Old Soggy out of the red and back to a normal operating level. Bringing numbers one and four back to normal power, the three engines would carry our lightly loaded Fortress along with the formation.

I snuggled as tightly as possible into the security of the formation as our fifty-calibers hammered in defense. The enemy attacked in waves of nine planes firing simultaneously. Cannon shells from several of the Messerschmitts exploded in our right wing, leaving mangled metal and gaping holes. Each man believed the wing would buckle and collapse. We visualized ourselves spinning earthward, trapped in our seats by the centrifugal force. But the shattered wing held and we breathed a silent sigh.

Within moments my copilot yelled, "Major, look at that wing!" I jerked another look at the right wing and saw great volumes of oil streaming from the rear of the number four engine.

"They've hit an oil-pressure line," I answered.

"That engine can't go very long like that," my copilot worried. He was right. Within minutes all the oil for that engine would be pumped overboard, and number four would smelt itself into molten steel and aluminum. I brought number one and Old Soggy to near maximum power as number four melted away and jerked to a frozen halt.

With just two engines, we would not be able to hold both altitude and speed. I elected to give up altitude in an attempt to maintain the speed of the formation. This might permit us to fly under the other B-17s. Like an umbrella, they would prevent fighter attacks from above. But we were a cripple and the German pilots knew it. They swarmed in from all sides like piranha, each taking a small bite, dashing away to safety, and then lashing back for another bite. We were being eaten alive.

They no longer attacked in waves. Each enemy pilot wanted to get credit for the kill. They screamed in from all angles, each pressing his attack dangerously close to a collision in the hope of delivering the fatal shot. My gunners were doing a good job, but they were no match for the heavily armed and highly maneuverable fighters. Our only hope was to reach the fighter escort rendezvous point. Just a little longer and we would be there.

The German fighters were no match for our P-51s and they knew it. If they would abandon the fight, we just might nurse our injured bird home on two engines. We only needed to make it to the rendezvous point, but now we were several thousand feet below the formation, and well behind. The formation could not slow and descend to protect us.

There is nothing more inviting to a fighter pilot than a lone crippled bomber. Eighteen enemy fighters tried to finish us off. The attacks intensified and they were getting the best of it. The top gunner and tailgunner were dead. The bombardier and other three gunners lay bleeding, near death. Not a single gun was manned. We were defenseless.

A terrible end seemed certain as enemy fire ripped and clawed at all sides of our airplane. They were blasting our bomber apart rivet by rivet. I marveled at its ability to hang together, but had accepted the fact that we were going to die. Then hope leaped through each of us as my copilot shouted on the intercom, "The P-51s! There they are! At eleven o'clock!" In his excitement, he pointed toward the tiny dots in the sky as if everyone on the ship could see his extended arm and finger.

We flew directly toward our fighters. "Come on, you guys. What are you waiting for?" I mumbled to our fighter escort still miles away. The Germans must have also seen the Mustangs coming because the attacks slackened. Just before turning tail, four of them took one last determined blast at us from ten o'clock. Bullets slashed through the ship and a pair of 20mm shells exploded in the left wing. The blasts destroyed the fuel control system to the number one engine. The damaged engine spun helplessly to a stop and raw fuel gushed out of the holes left by the exploding shells. Struggling to control the nearly powerless Fortress, I yelled to my copilot, "Get the fuel shut off to number one before we fireball." While he closed the necessary valves, I brought Old Soggy up to maximum power again.

As the Messerschmitts scrambled back toward the safety of Germany, a fresh and shiny Mustang eased into tight formation on each wingtip. By lowering their flaps and landing gear, they could chug along at the slow airspeed our mangled Fortress was making. One of the Mustang pilots, not knowing my rank, called on the mission frequency, "Colonel, you got a dead bird there. You guys going to bail out?"

Five of my crewmen would not survive a bailout and we would not abandon our dead comrades, so returning the promotion, I answered, "No, Colonel, I've got one good engine, 22,000 feet, and I'm headed in the right direction. I think we'll just stay with it."

"Well, sir," came the reply, "we own all the sky in this part of the world. There won't be no more fighter attacks, but the Krauts still own most of France down there. If you bail out here you might find a friendly Frenchman. The farther west you go, the closer you get to the German front line and that'll get you shot."

"That may be so, Colonel, but if we can go just a little bit farther than you think, we'll be on the U.S. side of the front line and that means safety." I argued.

"Now, you know you can't do that, Colonel. I'm sitting out here looking right up the tail pipe of your number three engine and it's glowing red hot and smoking worse than an uphill freight train. I wouldn't give it more than ten minutes before it splatters itself all over the sky. You're going to be flying a very heavy glider."

"You may be right, Colonel, but even that beats walking. Will you stay with us to report our down position?"

"Roger, and good luck."

We needed to lighten our load to remain aloft. Those who could work started dumping everything overboard. They dumped the guns, the ammo, the tools, the flak suits, excess clothing—anything and everything that could lighten our load by the least pound. We stripped her clean. Holding the Fortress close to the best glide speed, I glanced at the engine gauges. All the needles lay lifeless against their numbered faces except those labeled number three. Old Soggy's needles all pointed to the big numbers in the red.

How things had changed since that morning. We had planned to red-line Old Soggy to death and now we were red-lining it in the hope of saving our lives. We had wanted to destroy Old Soggy, but now we all prayed that this tired and abused warrior would hang together.

Old Soggy thrashed on. It clamored and banged beyond those three minutes prescribed by the manufacturer. It shuddered and smoked beyond the ten minutes prescribed by our fighter escort pilot. It charged on past the time that even my hopeful crew dared dream of. As we gradually traded altitude for distance, we neared the front line. We were low enough to see individual artillery blasts and began to worry about small arms fire from the ground. I pushed the mike button and said, "I want to thank you two peashooters for following us down, but I think you had better break off and head for home."

A pleading reply came quickly, "Now, Colonel! We ain't fired a shot all day. We're still fully armed. We can suppress some of the ground fire for you."

"Not on your life! You start shooting at those Krauts, and they're going to shoot back. If you guys just back off and get out of sight, they'll think we're going to crash. I'm hoping they won't waste a shot on us."

"Well, sir, it's your mule so I guess you can pull the plow any way you want. You come see me in Nashville after the war." With that and a hand salute, the two P-51 pilots cleaned up their Mustangs and streaked for altitude and home. We were alone. Old Soggy would be the difference between safety or capture—possibly the difference between life or death.

At 6,000 feet we could make out various German vehicles and an occasional cluster of men. I wondered what they thought as they looked up and saw a battered B-17 beating painfully along at low altitude on one bleeding engine. By now, Old Soggy was blowing so much oil and smoking so badly that, from the ground, it probably appeared that we were on fire. Not one shot was fired at us as we struggled to preserve our precious little altitude.

At 4,000 feet we were in the bloody battle zone between the two armies. At 2,000 feet we began to recognize GIs in U.S. Army battle dress. At 1,000 feet we saw that all vehicles below us had stars and bars, instead of swastikas.

I lined up with the largest clearing that was straight ahead and prepared for the landing. It would have to be good the first time. There would be no second chance. The gear whined into down-and-locked, the flaps chattered into position, and Old Soggy groaned with the additional drag. At the edge of the field, I let up on Old Soggy just a little for the first time in an hour. The Fortress half wallowed and half flopped into an otherwise routine landing. We were safe now and I eased Old Soggy into idle-cutoff.

After seeing our injured crewmen ambulanced away, the remainder of the crew gathered under the still-smoking number three engine. Old Soggy sizzled and creaked with thermal contractions. We looked at it in amazement and appreciation, speechless.

It was about a week later in England when the chief of our ground crew came to me and said, "Good news, Major. Headquarters has decided that your airplane is good enough to fix up and fly out of that field. They've given me four new engines to put on it and—"

"You'll only need three, Sergeant," I interrupted.

"What do you mean, sir?"

"I just logged an hour of single-engine B-17 time behind the best darn engine in the Army. If you so much as touch one wrench to that engine, I'll write Old Soggy across your chest with my 45."

"But, sir! There wasn't a drop of oil left in the number three tank. We're entitled to a new engine."

"Sergeant, you just get some oil, put it in that tank, and keep your mouth shut. Do you understand?" I growled.

Bewildered, confused, and a little unhappy, the sergeant answered, "Yes, sir," and departed with the recovery crew to get our Fortress.

Old Soggy flew five more missions before dying a hero's death. By the time of Old Soggy's last mission, the German fighters no longer chewed on all sides of a B-17. They decided that a frontal attack, attempting to kill the pilots, was the most effective way to stop a Fortress. A group of ten or more fighters would come streaking in nose-to-nose with a B-17, fire a fierce barrage, and pull up at the last moment. During one such attack, one of the German fighter pilots rolled left as he pulled up, but he got too much roll and not enough pull. His left wing smashed squarely into Old Soggy. Both the fighter and Old Soggy exploded into each other. Only mangled pieces of Old Soggy hung from its shattered mount.

We repeatedly looked toward Old Soggy only to look away in disbelief. We had come to think of Old Soggy as one of the indestructible constants in our world of ever-escalating destruction. It never occurred to us that Old Soggy would one day be gone. It was inconceivable that our Fortress could even fly without Old

Soggy, but the reality was there. It was there in the twisted wreckage surrounding the number three engine position. It was there in the failure to feel and hear a familiar balky, uneven response to movement of the number three engine controls. As we gradually accepted the fact that Old Soggy was gone, a somber silence fell upon the crew. We recalled and relived the day Old Soggy struggled so desperately to save our lives. We had lost a dear and faithful friend.

Officially, Old Soggy was credited with completing 87 missions, saving one B-17 and its crew, and downing one Messerschmitt. I thought the Distinguished Flying Cross was in order, but they don't give medals to engines.

RAINMAKER

T HE CONCEPT OF MAKING CLOUDS RELEASE THEIR moisture to fall to the earth as rain is now commonplace, but I believe the original idea was hatched by Bo Wages in the spring of 1934. The drought that led Bo to the idea had been slowly building in Texas. Through most of 1933 there was very little rainfall and things were looking pretty grim. Then came 1934, perhaps the worst drought year on record. Suffering and economic loss was immense.

Drought is a terrible thing. It slowly drains the rivers and lakes, and then dries up the water wells. With this mischief done, it blisters the land and lets the wind steal it away. Crops and live-stock suffer immeasurably. Most of all, it makes people desperate. In order to avoid total losses, Texas farmers and ranchers were willing to try anything. Some even enticed various Indians to perform rain dances, but with disappointing results. The time was right for an imaginative and resourceful person.

I could tell that Bo had been lost in some engrossing thought for the past few days. He hadn't shouted at me, slammed the stick against my leg, or kicked the rudder pedals as a reminder to coordinate the controls. In fact, he was so quiet that I even looked back once to see if he had fallen out of the rear cockpit during some of my boyish gyrations. No, there he was. He was gazing at the clouds. Upon landing, I probed, "I must be getting good at this flying since you ain't yelling at me no more."

"No, boy, you ain't a bit better than you were last week. I've just had something more important on my mind."

"What's more important than flying?"

"I been thinking about the farmers and ranchers out in west Texas. They're desperate and would pay plenty for a little rain."

"No doubt about that, Bo. We could use some rain here too," I agreed.

"Well, what would you say if I told you that I figured out how to make it rain?"

"I'd say you're nuts. Nobody can make it rain. It just rains when it gets good and ready," I lectured.

"Not necessarily, boy. It can be ready like a loaded and cocked pistol, but if nobody pulls the trigger, nothing happens. Now you look at that cloud up there," Bo said, pointing out a large, billowy cumulus. "There's a million gallons of water up there, boy, but the trigger never gets pulled and so it just stays up there in the sky. Well, I've figured out how to pull the trigger."

"How are you going to do that?"

"You got to know 'meterlology,' boy. It's a science. I don't know it all, but I do know that all bad weather, meaning rain mostly, comes from low pressure. When a hurricane comes boiling up out of the Gulf and hits the coast, the barometer drops like the dickens. Or when a tornado spins by, the bottom just falls out. And all cold and warm fronts come out of low-pressure systems. It's the low pressure that does it, boy!"

I didn't have the least idea what Bo was talking about, but his tone indicated that he was firmly convinced and that was enough for me. "So how are you going to make it rain?" I asked.

"Simple, boy. We just lower the pressure."

My mind fumbled with the bits and pieces Bo had fed it. I tried to group them into a meaningful whole but failed. Before I could formulate the all-important question, "How?" Bo volunteered, "A lot of people know all about clouds and moisture, and a lot of them know about pressure, but none of them know how to lower the pressure inside a cloud. That's the hard part, boy, and I've got it figured out. We do it with dynamite!"

An even more bewildered look must have crossed my face because Bo explained, "You see, an explosion is nothing more than a ball of high pressure expanding outward very fast. As all that high-pressure air rushes out, it must leave behind a big vacuum, a big low-pressure area. Then all that air comes rushing back in to fill up that low pressure. So we're going to blow the moisture apart as a cloud, and when it comes rushing back into the low pressure, it's going to rain like the dickens," he proudly said.

After thinking about his idea for a while, I agreed that it did sound logical enough to justify a trial. We decided to ask my father if we could experiment on some of the clouds over our dairy pastures.

"Are you out of your minds?" my father almost shouted. "Even if it worked, those explosions would ruin me. The cows would stop giving milk. No sir, not around here you don't." He sounded final.

"Why, Mr. Hawkins, if this works, you won't need them cows. My plan has always been to cut you in for half since you've been so good to me." Bo countered.

"Half, you say?" Father was a good businessman and could see the potential profits in a parched state like Texas. "How much do you think it will make?"

"Well, I'm not real sure because nobody's ever done this before, but I hear they're paying them Indians $10 to dance and another $40 if it rains. That's $50. I think we could dynamite four pastures a day."

"That's $200 a day!" my father marveled. In 1934, $200 was more than he made in a whole month of milking cows. He was enticed. "I suppose it's worth a try, Bo, but I want to get all my cows down to the south pasture just after milking. You go up on the north end for your test. That'll give us about two miles between my cows and your explosions."

It was settled. We were to choose a day when we had a good cumulus structure, the wind was from the south, and all the cows had been freshly milked and moved to the south pasture. The part that Bo had failed to tell my father was that I would be the bombardier.

The day finally arrived. There was a south wind and fat cumulus clouds hanging heavy with moisture extended from 2,000 feet to about 9,000 feet. The milking was complete and the cows had been moved to the south pasture. In anticipation of the day,

Bo obtained a box of dynamite containing sixteen sticks. Resembling huge firecrackers, each stick had a fuse about eighteen inches long. Bo wasn't sure how many trial drops it would take to get the blast in the heart of a cloud so he said, "Take all sixteen sticks along in your lap."

Bo's job was to maneuver the airplane to the desired spot above the cloud. My job was to place the fuse into the flaming exhaust of the V-8 and drop the dynamite into the cloud. After the explosion, we planned to dive down below the cloud and fly through the rain.

On the first pass, we skimmed directly over the selected cloud. Our wheels almost touched the billowy white tops. Bo shouted, "Now! Now!"

I lit the fuse, dropped the dynamite and waited with uncertainty. After what seemed a very long time, there came a distantly muffled BLOOOM and a gentle rocking of the biplane. With its long fuse, the dynamite had fallen completely through the cloud and exploded on the ground. We went to a higher altitude to repeat our experiment.

Bo climbed some 2,000 feet above the cloud. The homemade biplane with its little Ford engine was straining for an altitude that is rarely attained. Using the same length of fuse from this altitude, our next stick of dynamite should explode in the center of the cloud. When directly over the cloud, I lit the fuse and dropped the stick. Peering over the edge of the cockpit, I watched the dynamite fall. We heard the blast and saw the plume expand north of the cloud; we missed the entire cloud. "It's our speed," Bo shouted against the noise of the open cockpit. "Drop it sooner!"

We dropped higher. We dropped sooner. We dropped upwind and we dropped downwind, but after five attempts we still hadn't hit the cloud. We adjusted our altitude for the length of fuse, our drop point for the speed of the airplane, and our direction of approach for the wind, but we were still denied success. There were too many variables.

The problem of precision high-altitude bombardment would not be solved until World War II and the Norden bombsight, but Bo was determined. Shouting against the slipstream, he said, "Too much free fall. Too much time for the wind. Cut the fuse in half."

Working with a nine-inch fuse allowed us to fly closer to the cloud and reduce the free fall, but as the afternoon progressed, the wind increased, and the turbulence around the cloud worsened.

With eight sticks gone, and using every trick Bo could think of, we had only grazed the cloud once. Bo was angered. He suddenly realized that each attempt thus far had been with nine-inch or longer fuses, and from straight and level flight. Trying to describe a new scheme, he shouted: "Four-inch fuse. Four-inch fuse and dive bomb. Dive bomb."

It's very difficult for a boy to argue with a man thirty years his senior while seated in the wind-whipped front cockpit of a roaring biplane. I didn't want to try the dive bombing but couldn't tell him. It wouldn't have done any good if I were able to tell him because Bo was obsessed. He circled high above the cloud and nosed over into the dive. I laid my knife edge across the fuse at the four-inch length and was surprised about how short that really was. As we neared the cloud in a steep dive, I cheated a little and cut the fuse to five inches. Placing the fuse near the exhaust pipe, I waited for Bo's command.

"Now! Now!" Bo shouted.

I struck the fuse into the exhaust pipe flame, saw that it was lit and let the dynamite slide overboard. I leaned right to get a glimpse of the dynamite as it fell, and my heart and mind were penetrated by sudden and terrifying fear. The dynamite was buoyed in the wake of the lower wing and was diving in close formation with the biplane. Bo must have seen what was happening, too, because I felt him roll left and pull up hard. I clenched my eyelids and shrunk into the cockpit. There was an enormous, crackling sharp BLAAM that punished my ears. A brilliant flash of orange light and sudden heat engulfed the biplane. The airplane trembled all over and violently jerked into a cartwheel motion. We were spinning out of control.

During the gyrations, the remaining seven sticks of dynamite spilled from my lap and scattered through the belly of the biplane. I struggled to retrieve the dynamite but was hampered by the control stick being wildly thrust around by Bo. He was desperately trying to regain control of the tumbling, falling airplane. I couldn't reach the dynamite and Bo couldn't regain control. The blast had blown away the right horizontal stabilizer and elevator. We were burning and we were going to crash.

Trailing a stream of orange flame and blue-gray smoke, we neared the ground in a tumbling, spinning motion. I tugged hard to tighten my seat belt, braced my feet on the instrument panel, closed my eyes, and wrapped my arms around my head. Just prior to the crash, I heard the engine surge to full power and felt the stick slam hard left. I thought it would be over in an instant, but the sounds of the impact seemed to go on and on.

Snapping, crunching, grinding, bumping, banging, and popping, continued as we tumbled across the earth. Then, suddenly, it stopped as we came to rest. The only sound was the hissing steam spraying from the ruptured radiator. I opened my eyes slowly and found that we were engulfed in a dense cloud of swirling dust and smoke. Then alarm spread rapidly through my body as the penetrating odor of gasoline reached my nostrils. From behind me came, "Get out, boy, get out! We're on fire!"

Being small and agile, I had the seat belt off and squeezed through the tangled structure as Bo took a breath to add, "Run, boy, run!" I was running like a frightened deer when the remaining seven sticks detonated. The blast was fierce. It propelled me through the air and then slammed me to the ground. Pain pierced each eardrum. I instinctively curled into a tight ball as chunks of grass and earth showered about me. I rolled over on my stomach and looked back toward the biplane. There was no airplane and there was no Bo.

"No! No!" I shouted, rejecting the idea that Bo could be gone. Springing to my feet, I fought back the thought of such a loss and raced toward the crash site. There was nothing but a large crater where the wreckage of the biplane had been. Standing on the edge of the crater, I could see bits and pieces of the biplane, but no sign of its pilot. Tears began to well up in my eyes and my breath came in short, difficult gasps as I stared at the bottom of the crater. Then through the still swirling dust came, "Oohhhh."

My spirits soared. I dashed in the direction of the sound and found Bo lying on his back, submerged in a pile of dirt and grass. Most of his clothing had been blown away by the blast. He was bleeding from numerous cuts and punctures. Kneeling beside him, I brushed the debris away and asked, "Bo, are you hurt bad?"

Grimacing through obvious pain he said, "No, boy, I'll be all right. Did you feel any raindrops?"